# FOREWORD

For business owners desperate to take their companies public, reverse mergers are in fact a cheaper, quicker alternative to an IPO. They're also more certain. Unlike a traditional IPO, a reverse merger doesn't depend on market conditions, so it happens on schedule, come bull or bear.

# Table of Content

# Chapter 1

## GOING PUBLIC: ADVANTAGES & DISADVANTAGES

### The Reverse Merger

Often new clients come to us having already decided that they want to go public. Before we turn on the jets, we sit them down and discuss the advantages and disadvantages of going public to ensure that they are making an informed decision. Here's what we talk about.

In a Reverse Merger the private company shareholders purchase control of the public shell company and then merge it with their private company. The private company shareholders receive a substantial majority of the shares of the public company and control of its board of directors. The transaction can be accomplished within weeks, resulting in the private company becoming a public company. If the shell is a Reporting SEC registered Company, the private company does not go through an expensive and time consuming review process with state and federal regulators because the public company has already completed the process. The transaction involves the private and shell company exchanging information on each other, negotiating the merger terms, and signing a share exchange agreement. At the closing the shell company issues a substantial majority of its shares and board control to the shareholders of the private company, who pay for the shell and contribute their private company shares to the shell company they now control. This share exchange and change of control completes the Reverse Merger and the private company is now public.

# Advantage

## Access to Capital

Emerging growth technology companies often have limited access to capital. The fact that their assets walk out the door at the end of every working day makes it very difficult to obtain financing from banks or other traditional sources. However, technology companies often need significant amounts of capital to maximize the development and/or marketing of their technology through an invariably limited window of opportunity. As a result, it is very difficult to build a technology company through cash flow - it is just too limited. The public markets allow technology companies with strong growth potential to raise the capital necessary to develop full speed ahead. Once the company is public, subsequent financings are easier as the company has a track record with investors and the securities regulators.

## Liquidity

A shareholder of a company that has gone public and listed its securities on a stock exchange or over-the-counter system (like Nasdaq) can sell his or her shares through the public market. This is called liquidity. Prior to a company going public it is very difficult, if not impossible, for the shareholders to sell their shares. Being able to provide shareholders with liquidity makes it much easier to attract investment into the company, as the investors have a built-in exit strategy. Liquidity also gives the principals of the company the ability to cash out their equity position in the company.

## Public Company Multiples

Public company shares are usually valued at a higher price than a comparative private company. This is because of the fact that there is an organized market through which the shares may be sold. This is usually referred to as the "public company multiple".

## Incentive Stock Options

High tax rates and cost of living, a de-valued dollar, and intense competition make it very difficult for the technology companies to attract and retain experienced management and technical personnel, especially from the United States. One partial solution to this problem is the granting of incentive stock options. Public emerging growth technology companies are often able to attract the people they need by providing them with a reasonable salary coupled with a substantial number of incentive stock options. These options grant the employee or consultant the right to buy a certain number of shares of the company at the market price of the shares at the date of the grant for a specified period. As the market price of the shares of the company (hopefully) climbs towards the heavens, the stock options become worth a significant amount of money.

Many companies use stock and stock option plans to attract and retain talented employees. It is increasingly common to recruit and compensate executives with a combination of salary and stock. Stock in a public company can be issued as a performance based reward or incentive.

This reward could be deemed desirable if the stock has a public market. Stock can be instrumental in attracting and keeping key personnel. Also, certain tax advantages are a consideration when issuing stock to an employee. Generally, capital gains taxes are lower than ordinary income taxes. Owners and employees may have specific restrictions relating to the liquidity and sale of the stock.

A public offering can create a market for the company's stock. This market can result in liquidity and reward for the company's employees. A stock plan for employees demonstrates corporate good will allow employees to become partial owners in the company where they work.

An allocation of ownership or division of equity can lead to increased productivity, morale and loyalty. This type of compensation is a way of connecting an employee's financial future to the company's success.

## Acquisitions

In today's rapidly changing world, technology companies often have to grow quickly in order to survive. One method of achieving rapid growth is to grow by acquisition. Often the most expeditious way to deal with a competitor, or potential competitor, is to buy it. Public companies can use their stock, instead of their cash, to make acquisitions. This is sometimes referred to as using your stock as "currency". Further, the markets provide public companies with a ready valuation for their stock. A valuation of a private company often reflects illiquidity. A successful public offering will increase a company's valuation leading to a variety of opportunities for mergers and acquisitions. With the ability to raise additional capital by returning to the public markets for another offering, a public company is better able to finance a cash acquisition.

A public company also has the advantage of using the market's valuation when exchanging stock in an acquisition. SEC disclosure requirements offer merger candidates the assurance of shareholder scrutiny and accurate reporting of the financial condition or solvency of the public company. Using stock to acquire another company can be easier and less expensive than other methods.

Additionally, Many private firms do not appear on the radar screen of potential acquirers. Being public makes it easier for other companies to notice and evaluate the firm for potential synergies.

## Profile & Prestige

There is no question that taking a technology company public increases its profile. The increased profile assists the company in attracting investors, strategic partners, and customers. As people come to understand the company's product they will be much

4

more likely to purchase its stock. People buy what they understand. Further, people often presume that public companies are more substantial than private companies.

A public offering of stock can help a company gain prestige by creating a perception of stability. A company's founders, co-founders and managers gain an enormous amount of personal prestige from being associated with a client that goes public. Prestige can be very helpful in recruiting key employees and marketing products and services.

When sharing ownership with the public, you spread the company's reputation and increase its business opportunities. By selling stock on an exchange your company can gain additional exposure and become better known. This exposure may lead to improved recognition and business operations.

The public status can be leveraged when marketing goods and services. Often a company's suppliers and consumers become shareholders, which may encourage continued or increased business. In this example, a public company could have a competitive advantage over a private enterprise. Going public can indicate credibility to a company's customers, which may lead to increased sales and a greater corporate profile.

Once public, lenders and suppliers may perceive the company as a safer credit risk, enhancing the opportunities for favorable financing terms. Also, a public offering can create publicity that is effective when marketing your company.

## Publicity

Public companies are more likely to receive the attention of major newspapers, magazines and periodicals than a private enterprise. The proper use of press releases, interviews or news stories can increase investor awareness, shareholder value and demand for the stock.

A strong ad campaign coupled with media initiatives can potentially increase sales and revenue. The publicity received from a public offering encourages new business development and strategic alliances. Analyst reports and daily stock market tables contribute to the awareness of the consumer and financial community.

A successful public offering can get your company's story out to the world and open an opportunity for investors that are not suited for an investment in a private company. The publicity that a public offering brings can attract the attention of potential partners or merger candidates.

• **Corporate Income Tax Shelter:** Many shell companies have what is known as a tax-loss carry forward. This means that a loss incurred in previous years can be applied to income in future years. When this occurs, the future income is sheltered from income taxes. Since most active public companies become dormant public companies through a string of losses, or at least one large one, there's a better than average chance the shell you meet will offer this opportunity.

## Exit Strategy

One of the important benefits of a public offering is the fact that the company's stock eventually becomes liquid, offering reward and financial freedom for the founders and employees.

The fact that the company becomes public provides a potential exit strategy and liquidity to the investors. A psychological sense of financial success can be an added benefit of going public. The fact that the company goes public can enhance the personal net worth of a company's shareholders.

Even if a public company's shareholders do not realize immediate profits, public-traded stock can be used as collateral to secure loans.

Although it is a bad signal to investors when an entrepreneur sells his own shares, it still makes sense for many entrepreneurs to cash out some of their equity in order to diversify their holdings or to enjoy life. After all, isn't that why you started your company?

## Future Capital

Once public, firms can easily go back to the public markets to raise more cash. Of course, it is all based on the performance of the company. The company with average performance will have a hard time to raise more capital.

## Disadvantages

### Time commitment

Prior to going public, technology companies are often achieving a high growth rate with a thin management structure. Everyone already has a great deal on their plate. The going public process requires a large commitment of management's time and energy and it takes management's focus off the company's core business. Once the company has carried out its going public process and listed its shares on an exchange, a portion of management's time will be taken up dealing with regulatory requirements and generating market interest in the company.

### Expense to obtain and maintain

Professional advisors, such as lawyers and accountants, must be extensively involved in the going public process in order for the company to avoid costly errors. The total costs to carry out a reverse merger can vary from 300,000 to 1,000,000 U.S. dollars. Once a company is listed on an exchange, it must continue to retain professional advisors in order to ensure that it complies with the complex requirements of the securities regulatory regime.

### Disclosure requirements

When a company goes public it must comply with the disclosure rules. Simply put, the company has to do the "Full Monty". Many aspects of the company's business, such as its financial performance, the terms of its material contracts, and the compensation it pays its executives, become a matter of public record and accessible to its competitors. This public disclosure of material changes as they occur can have a huge impact on a technology company's ability to compete against other private technology companies that are not forced to make such disclosure.

A major reason why firms resist going public is the loss of confidentiality in company operations and policies. For example, a company could be destroyed if the company were to disclose its technology or profitability to its competitors.

### Regulatory scrutiny

Junior listed companies are required to seek the prior consent of the stock exchange upon which their shares are listed before carrying out many common activities, such as issuing shares and acquiring assets. Most entrepreneurs find it frustrating to have to go to the time and expense of seeking consent to carry out activities that they previously undertook without the consent of third parties. This process is particularly difficult for technology companies that are in areas of business that are not readily understood by the securities regulators.

### Investor relations

While a public market for a company's shares provides a mechanism for valuing the company on a daily basis, a company's share price can become too much of a focal point. This can be a distraction for employees owning shares or options and can result in management decisions being made to focus on the short term to boost the share price rather than to strengthen the company in the long term. While a public listing may hold the promise of enhanced liquidity, it is up to the company to generate market demand for its shares. Companies that are listed on junior exchanges generally cannot attract the attention of analysts or the press and must seek assistance from investor relations experts or develop the expertise in-house. This kind of advice can be expensive and often does not result in immediate tangible results. This is also an area where unscrupulous players can seriously impact a company's credibility in the marketplace if they are not properly monitored by management.

## Profit-sharing

If the firm is sitting on a highly successful venture, future success (and profit) has to be shared with outsiders. After the reverse merger, a significant portion of company's stake goes to the outsiders. Being private, the founders of the company do not need to share profit with outsiders.

## Reporting and Fiduciary Responsibilities

Public companies must continuously file reports with the SEC and the exchange they list on. They must comply with certain state securities laws ("blue sky"), NASD and exchange guidelines. This disclosure costs money and provides information to competitors.

## Loss of Control

Outsiders are often in a position to take control of corporate management and might even fire the entrepreneur/company founder. While there are effective anti-takeover measures, investors are not willing to pay a high price for a company in which poor management could not be replaced.

## Summary

Going public is not for every company. The directors of the company must weigh the advantages of going public against the disadvantages before making the decision to proceed to carry out a reverse merger procedure.

# Chapter 2

## THE STEPS OF A REVERSE MERGER TRANSACTION

Before we talk about reverse merger, here are some key issues which we would like to clarify:

### Shell Profile:

The company was formed to be a vehicle for merger with a private company, and is free of operating history, assets or liabilities, existing or contingent.

### How Long Until Trading:

This process is demanding and time sensitive to both the client company and the public shell company. Assuming the co-operation of the client company in providing all necessary information, obtaining action of its Board of Directors and providing audited financial statements within the required time, you may expect to be trading in 60 to 90 days after execution of the agreement.

### The Cost:

The cost for the transaction is from $300,000 to $150,000.00, in U.S. Dollars, which includes legal fees.

### Progress Payments:

Progress payments are acceptable in three installments: The first due when work is commenced, the second when the SEC filing is made, and the final when the Form 211 is filed. If you cancel the engagement after preparation of the SEC filing is commenced, all of this fee will be retained. The firm who helped the process may also retain a minimum of 6% of the merged company.

## Steps for the Reverse Merger

If a reverse merger sounds like a good idea to you, here are the steps you need to take:

## The Four Key Steps to a Successful Reverse Merger

While there are numerous steps involved in successfully completing a "Reverse Merger" the process can be broken into four key steps. To give you an idea of what to expect during the reverse merger process, we will guide you through the four key steps to a successful reverse merger.

## Step One - Review Client Goals and Capital Structure

Before even identifying a suitable public shell to conduct a reverse merger, you ought to work with the client company's management to identify their short-term and long-term objectives and how they relate to the client's desire to "go public." This is probably the most important step of the reverse merger process.

During this step we need to review several aspects of the client's company and how they relate to the client's goals. In this step we will help the client identify and resolve individual issues that may have an impact on how the reverse merger will be accepted in the financial marketplace. We will also help develop a proper capital structure engineered to facilitate the client's goals, including future fund raising activities, acquisition prospects, stock options and warrants, employee stock ownership programs (ESOPs), stock management issues, and so forth.

**Devise your financing strategy.** A reverse merger is an indirect route to raising capital. Entrepreneurs must first consider how additional capital will be raised after the deal is done.

A public company can issue and exercise warrants. Some public shell companies already have warrants issued and outstanding; some have previously registered the underlying common stock shares with the Securities and Exchange Commission—which is a significant benefit. This is much easier and much more valuable to a company that wants to raise capital with warrants. If the newly public company must create and issue warrants, the road to getting them exercised will be trickier but still possible. In short, exercising warrants where the underlying common shares are not registered requires the assistance of a brokerage firm and must occur in a state where there is no registration requirement for issuance of shares of up to $1 million.

If you are going the private-offering route (i.e., an offering sold to select individuals rather than through a sale directly to the public at large), the deal must be carefully structured. Specifically, the amount of stock owned by investors that the new owners do not know and cannot influence must be diminished so that a stable quote can be established. Usually, this is done by reducing the percentage of the total number of shares these investors own. By doing so, as an added incentive, the private investors can be offered stock at a discount to the market price.

Without a strategic plan the reverse merger will inevitably fail at some point in the future.

## Step Two - Identify a Suitable Public Shell

Depending on the client's goals, strategies and budget, we will help select an appropriate public shell vehicle. There are numerous types of public shells available. Some are trading, some are not trading. Some report to the Securities and Exchange Commission while others remain non-reporting. Some even have cash on hand and are looking for just the right private operating company to conduct a reverse merger.

**Start with a clean shell.** As was mentioned, many shells are created for the express purpose of merging with a private company. These shells have no predecessor entities and, as a result, little baggage in the way of a business failure or other skeletons in the closets.

You can find one by contacting the usual suspects. As a first stop, ask an attorney. Every metropolitan area has a law firm with a securities practice. Often, these firms have a dormant public company sitting on one of the partners' bookshelves.

Another alternative is an accountant. People who control shell companies tend to keep the financial statements, such as they are, up to date. This brings accountants into the loop. Like attorneys, they know where the bodies are.

Another source is financing consultants. In fact, many actually have a couple of shell corporations and, upon request, can manufacture a clean public shell. A made-to-order shell without the baggage of a business failure in its background can sometimes be the way to go.

But there's often a cost involved. That is, you will most likely end up with the financing consultants as minority shareholders in the new company, holding between 2 percent and 5 percent. However, in almost any reverse merger transaction, the principals of the shell company keep a small equity position in the company going forward. Therefore, this surrender of equity is simply a cost of doing business.

**Check your greed.** The great rallying cry of the 1980s, popularized by the Hollywood oily takeover artist Gordon Gekko, "Greed is good," doesn't apply with a reverse merger. It's possible to structure a reverse merger so that at the end of the day, the public owns 2 percent of the company and the remaining 98 percent is controlled by the owners of the private company that acquired the shell. Unfortunately, there's almost no incentive for any other investors to become involved if the only people who truly benefit are the insiders. The lesson is, if you plan to involve the public with the intention of engaging in a truly symbiotic relationship, you simply must leave some value on the table.

## Step Three - Prepare and File All Required Documents

First and foremost, unless the client wishes to reverse merge into a non-reporting public shell such as a NQB Pink Sheet shell company, then the client will need to obtain a proper audit conducted by a licensed public accounting firm.

Unfortunately, there's a stigma attached to reverse mergers. LVA-Vision, a company that owns free-standing centers offering laser refractive eye surgery, founder Jerry Stephens, who used the technique to brilliant effect, said that although it worked for his company, "there's definitely another side to these deals. If it wasn't for my long-standing reputation in the medical community, our deal might have been perceived differently." Largely, the bad rap stems from the fact that reverse mergers are not understood, Stephens says.

Entrepreneurs contemplating such a transaction can and should take steps to elevate the profile of their "new" company. Specifically:

**Hire a national accounting firm.** One of the reasons the Big Five fees are high is because they inspire a lot of comfort among investors, traders, and regulators. If you saved a lot on fees at the front end, this might be worth investing in on the back end.

**Hire a prestigious law firm.** It's almost a certainty that the attorney who initially helps you with your reverse merger transaction, if he or she is an expert in these kinds of deals, will not be with a prestigious downtown law firm. However, after the offering is completed, you should consider retaining one of these firms. Why? When deciding whether to get involved in your offering, many investors and brokers will judge your firm by the company it keeps. An unknown law firm makes a neutral to negative impression. But a well-known and powerful law firm sends an unmistakable message.

## Step Four - Become a Public Entity

Once all of the required legal documents have been executed, filed and seen through to completion, the client will successfully have taken over the public shell vehicle and transitioned itself into a publicly traded corporation.

## Examples of Successful Reverse Mergers

In 1970, Ted Turner acquired control of Rice Broadcasting (WJRJ-TV) in Atlanta, Georgia. Eventually this company became Turner Broadcasting and was acquired by Time/Warner and later merged with America Online. Ted Turner is now one of the wealthiest men in the world.

In 1996, Muriel Siebert, the first woman to purchase a seat on the New York Stock Exchange (NYSE), reverse merged her discount brokerage house, Muriel Siebert & Co., into J. Michaels, Inc., a defunct, but publicly traded Brooklyn furniture company. The stock has since traded over $70 a share.

In 1999, Tony Robbins, best selling author of "Awakening the Giant Within", conducted a reverse merger with GHS, Inc. whose stock soared from $0.75 to over $12 a share.

Other well known companies that can trace their roots back to a successful reverse merger with a public shell include Blockbuster Entertainment, Inc., Occidental Petroleum Corporation, Waste Management, Inc., and RadioShack Corporation.

# Chapter 3

## COSTS AND TIMING OF A REVERSE MERGER

### Condensed Timetable

Surprisingly few companies can hope to negotiate their way through the tortuous process of a regular IPO, which can drag on for a year or more, from when the idea pops into the chief executive's head until he or she actually gets a check. Unfortunately, when

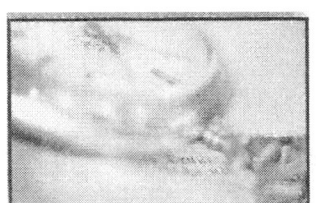 a company transitions from an entrepreneurial venture to a real public company fit for outside ownership, senior management's time is at its most valuable. Time spent in seemingly endless meetings and drafting sessions can have a disastrous effect on the growth upon which the offering is predicated, and even nullify it. In addition, during the many months it takes to put together an IPO, market conditions can deteriorate, closing the "IPO window" on a company. Over the past five years, the number of days for a company in registration has doubled, with the few IPOs that made it to market in 2001 averaging 159 days in registration^. During this time, management will spend an inordinate amount of time in meetings and drafting sessions, having a disastrous effect on the growth the offering is predicated on. In addition, during the many months it takes to put together an IPO, market conditions can deteriorate, closing the IPO window on a company. In contrast, a reverse merger can be completed in 60 to 90 days.

## Substantial Savings

An IPO involves substantial expense, including underwriting fees, legal fees, accounting fees, printing costs, and filing fees. For example, estimated expenses for a $60 million initial public offering consisting of 3,750,000 newly issued shares of common stock at $16.00 per share, can run between $5 to $6 million'. Compared to IPO, the cost of reverse merger is from $300,000 to $150,000.00, in U.S. Dollars, which is a substantial savings.

## Unaffected by Market Conditions

Over the past 5 years, there has been a dramatic decrease in IPOs, with 2001 activity at the lowest point in over 10 years due to the market conditions. In a conventional IPO, issuers exercise surprisingly little control over the timing of when they become public. But a reverse merger is impervious to market conditions. The deal rests on whether the shell company likes your company enough to be acquired by it - market conditions have almost no bearing.

## Shorter Track Record Required

While an IPO in today's market requires a relatively long and stable earnings history, the lack of an earnings history does not prevent a privately-held company without this track record from completing a reverse merger..

# Chapter 4

## REVERSE MERGER VS. AN IPO

The recent decline in technology stock prices these years has made it more challenging for the hi-tech companies to find underwriters for their initial public offerings. It is even more difficult for the small and medium sized companies to go public via IPO. The window of opportunity for an IPO was closed for many companies, and an underwriter's willingness to go forward with a particular IPO depends heavily on the current conditions of the stock market.

The difficulties in finding underwriters in today's market have increasingly lead the hi-tech companies to seek out alternative methods of going public. One of the most common alternatives is the reverse merger. While such non-traditional methods of going public have become more common over the last year, counsel for a company contemplating a reverse merger must be aware of the advantages and disadvantages of each option, and what steps must be taken to ensure that all appropriate regulatory rules are complied with.

A significant number of companies have gone public through reverse mergers in recent years. In a typical reverse merger, a privately operating company locates a dormant publicly trading company and the two companies agree to merge. As part of the merger transaction, the shareholders of the privately held company receive freely trading shares of the public company's stock. Once the merger is completed the business operations of the privately held company are carried out through the public corporation. In most cases, the name of the publicly traded company is changed to reflect the new business focus of the company.

In addition, the new management of the publicly traded company will attempt to arrange for a market-maker to publicly quote the shares on the over-the-counter

Bulletin Board or, if the company qualifies, on the Nasdaq SmallCap. The Bulletin Board is a regulated quotation service that is operated by the National Association of Securities Dealers, while the Nasdaq is an electronic stock market with defined listing standards that must be met before an issuer's stock can be quoted. If a company succeeds in having its stock quoted on either the Bulletin Board or the Nasdaq, a liquid market for the stock can develop.

Companies that go public through a reverse merger rather than a traditional IPO do so for a number of reasons, but the most common reason is that the company may simply be unable to find an underwriter for its stock. This could be due to a company's size, its business plan or for other reasons. During 1998 and 1999, when underwriters were primarily interested in handling IPOs forcompanies in the Internet and e-commerce industries, companies that were in other more traditional industries found it difficult to find underwriters to bring them public.

By going public through a reverse merger, a private company could gain many of the advantages of being a publicly traded company, including the ability to use the company's stock to acquire other companies, and the possibility that a liquid market for the company's shares could develop.

The main drawback of a reverse merger is that new capital is not raised by the company as part of the transaction. Instead, the company hopes to develop a relationship with a market-maker and other broker-dealers so that capital can be more easily raised at a later date through the sale of company's stock. The lack of an immediate inflow of new capital to the company is a significant disadvantage of a reverse merger when compared to a traditional IPO.

## Counsel Involvement

Counsel for private companies must become involved with a proposed reverse merger transaction at the earliest stage possible. Regulators such as the Securities and Exchange Commission give heightened scrutiny to such transactions. In the 1980's the

19

stock of a number of companies that went public through reverse mergers became the target of various manipulation schemes.

However, in recent years a number of relatively large and reputable companies have gone public through reverse mergers. For example, Alford Refrigerated Warehouses Inc., the largest public refrigerated warehousing operation in the southwest United States, went public through a reverse merger in 1998. its stock currently trades on the Nasdaq SmallCap market.

Attorneys who represent private companies that are considering a reverse merger must be cautious. One of the most important responsibilities that counsel has is to ensure that all of the necessary due diligence has been performed. First, counsel must ensure that the proposed merger candidate is indeed a publicly reporting company under the Securities and Exchange Act of 1934. Further, counsel must ensure that the merger candidate is current in all of its filings with the Securities and Exchange Commission. Next, counsel must ascertain the public company's operating history. Towards this end, counsel must determine whether the public company was formed solely to seek out a private company for a merger, or whether it was once an operating company that now no longer conducts any active business.

One of the most important issues that counsel must address during the due diligence review is whether the publicly traded company has any existing or contingent liabilities. If the publicly traded company was formed in anticipation of completing a merger, it is likely to have little or no operating history, and its existing and contingent liabilities can be determined relatively easily.

In the case of a publicly traded company that was formerly an operating company, a significant amount of time will have to be spent performing due diligence. Often such companies have complex histories, and it is not uncommon to find that the company has previously filed bankruptcy. While the bankruptcy filing may give counsel a certain amount of comfort if the company's liabilities were discharged, the filings in bankruptcy court must be carefully reviewed to ensure that this is the case.

Prior to the consummation of a reverse merger, counsel for the private company should review a list of the shareholders of the publicly traded company. The transaction documents must clearly state what the capital structure of the entity will be post-merger and who the shareholders will be. In several unfortunate cases, shareholders in the post-merger company have been surprised to find previous shareholders of the publicly traded company asserting themselves in the new business or selling their stock in the open market once the merger is completed. Selling by previous shareholders can exert downward pressure on the price of the company's stock.

Typically, the actual legal documents that consummate the merger are prepared by the attorney for the public company. Counsel for the private company must carefully review the documents to ensure that accurately reflect the terms of the deal and the parties' intent. Counsel should also ensure that the publicly traded company has a current set of audited financial statements. Full disclosure documents must be filed with the SEC, and counsel must be sure to advise the client that all SEC filings must be cleared prior to the start of market trading. Typically, SEC Form 8-K is used to make a detailed filing with the SEC regarding the reverse merger transaction.

## Listing Issuer's Stock

Counsel for the private company should also be looking ahead to ensure that everything possible is done to obtain a market maker for the company's stock and that the stock is quoted either on the Nasdaq SmallCap or the over-the-counter Bulletin Board. These steps will help increase the likelihood that a liquid market will develop which, in turn, can help the company obtain future financing and provide a way in which the shareholders of the company can sell their shares if they so chose.

To be eligible to have its stock price quoted on the Bulletin Board, a company must be current in all of its SEC filings and must find a market-maker willing to list price quotes for the company's stock. The rules relating to the eligibility for quotation are set forth in NASD Rules 6530 and 6540. The requirement that all companies listed on the bulletin board be current in their SEC filings was approved by the SEC in Release No. 34-40878 (Jan. 4, 1999). If a company wants its stock listed on the Nasdaq it must meet several requirements, including a public float of 1 million shares and a market value of the public float of $5 million. It is preferable to have a company's stock listed in the Nasdaq SmallCap, if the issuer meets the listing requirements.

The primary reason to do a reverse merger is the greater number of financing options that become available to companies once they are public. Some of these include:

The issuance of additional shares in a secondary offering

Exercise of warrants. Warrants are options that give the holder the right to purchase additional shares in a company at predetermined prices. When many shareholders with warrants -- which a public company can easily issue -- exercise their option to purchase additional shares, the company receives an infusion of capital, as shown in the chart below.

Private Offerings. Many, many more investors will step up to the plate for a private offering of shares once they know there is some sort of mechanism in place for them to resell their shares if the company succeeds. Most investors realize that even a successful company may not be able to go public if market conditions are off. But a company that is already public ....that's a different story. If it succeeds, there is a greater likelihood of developing a market for its common stock that accurately represents the company and lets investors sell their shares.

**A Good Deal:** Even if the market crashes while you're working on your reverse merger, it probably won't kill your deal. For the shell company with a few assets and little or no story to tell, a good merger is good news and worth pursuing, no matter what market conditions are.

## The Drawbacks of a Reverse Merger

Reverse Mergers aren't for everyone, however. There are several drawbacks to this financing technique. Among the disadvantages:

requirement for audited financial statements;

required publication of corporate information;

required filings of periodic and episodic reports with the Securities and Exchange Commission;

increased rules and regulations governing management, corporate activities and shareholder relations.

**Shop Talk:** The controlling shareholders of a shell corporation will most likely insist on owning a small stake in the deal going forward. This "trailing interest" is simply a cost of doing business.

## A Case In Point

Perhaps the best use of a reverse merger was made by LVA Group. The Company's founder, Jerry Stephens, already had a profitable hospital-management business. But he saw an opportunity in free-standing centers offering laser refractive eye surgery to correct myopia, also known as nearsightedness. However, the process was awaiting FDA approval, according to Stephens. "The United States was a multibillion-dollar market."

To get ready, the Company laid plans for financing the roll-out of centers in the United States and bought part of a laser surgery center in Toronto, where the process was already legal.

Considering financing alternatives, Stephens believed he could cobble together an IPO but concluded that it was highly unlikely for a new and untested concept. What if the FDA approval were delayed?

But with a reverse merger, Stephens only had to convince the controlling shareholder of a public shell that the reward was worth the risk. And the controlling shareholder of a shell company Stephens was talking with happened to agree .

In the resulting deal, he bought stock in the shell company in exchange for LVA Group's assets. At the end of the day, Stephens had a majority position in the shell company, and the shell company had the operating assets of his company. The public company then changed its name to LVA-Vision to reflect the deal and the future course of the business

<

**Don't Forget:** A reverse merger is not an end in itself. It is a technique or tool that makes a company more financeable.

Two months after the deal, the FDA approved the laser refractive procedure used by LVA, and Stephens was off and running. Almost immediate^ he raised nearly $500,000 privately. He also used his publicly traded common stock to buy the remaining interest in the Toronto facility. The private capital he'd raised, combined with the favorable lease terms on surgical laser equipment, helped Stephens roll out seven new surgery centers in the South and Midwest. After a brief honeymoon on the National Association of Securities Dealers' Bulletin Board (OTC BB), LVA-Vision moved up to NASDAD's SmallCap.

In a climaxing deal, LVA used its stock to purchase a chain of refractive surgery centers from another company. To acquire the company, LVA issued several millions of its own shares and in return got the other company's 19 wholly owned and operated refractive surgery centers around the country. As a final bonus, the company that LVA bought had $10 million in the bank when the deal was inked.

Today, LVA-Vision is the largest provider of vision treatment procedures in the United States.

Going public is not for every company. The directors of the company must weigh the advantages of going public against the disadvantages before making the decision to proceed to carry out an initial public offering.

# Chapter 5

## BUSINESS PLAN

### The Business Plan

A professional investor will rarely consider investing in a company, unless the proposal is first presented in the form of a cohesive, well-written business plan. Only after evaluating the feasibility of this business plan will they invest the first dollar.

A business plan is a written presentation that carefully explains the business, its management team, its products or services, and its goals together with strategies for reaching the goals. The entrepreneur, or whoever writes the business plan will, in all probability, find it a painstaking process. But keep in mind, this is the selling tool, and it requires careful consideration of all the multiple facets of a start-up or business expansion. It cannot be written as an afterthought, and it should not be taken lightly. Check with any underwriter or professional investor anywhere in the country, and you'll hear horror stories about ill-conceived, poorly written, or sloppily put together business plans. As great as the company's potential may be, it is usually doomed to rejection before it can even get a foot in the door, if it has a poorly conceived business plan.

There are two basic purposes to a business plan. One is to present the company in an engaging way with interesting information on how the business will be run for the next three to five years* or possibly longer. The other, of course, is to raise the money to do so. There's no business without the bucks. The entrepreneur must put all the howsfand needs together in one neat package. The human and physical resources must effectively interrelate with the marketing, operational, and financial strategies of the company.

Unless an entrepreneur has magical powers of persuasion, this is not the time to try to fake it.

The business plan should be considered a vital sales tool for approaching any financial sources, investors or lenders. They will want to know that the plan has been carefully thought out by the management team. They will want to be convinced that the team has the skills and expertise needed to effectively manage the company and are prepared to seize opportunities and solve all problems that arise. That's why the business plan must be well-prepared, professional in tone, and persuasive in conveying the company's potential.

I can't stress too strongly a good business plan is the cornerstone of successful financing. If you want their money, you've got to give them a good reason to buy. The business plan is where you lay out the reasons. It doesn't have to be unduly lengthy or complicated. But it must be informative and relevant. It needs to maintain logic and order, and show the company as effectively positioned as a good investment.

More important, the business plan should be specifically directed to the funding source and satisfy its particular concerns. For example, you would orient and write the plan differently for presentation to a banker versus a venture capitalist, a fund manager, or a private investor. The venture capitalist would want to know what risks are involved, whereas the banker cares more about how good the security is while the fund manager would like to know the year to year growth rate of the net profit of the company. These concerns must be individually addressed. There are no hard-and-fast rules for preparing a business plan. The key word is ingenuity. Strive for inventiveness. Strive to be interesting.

Here are some general guidelines covering the basic elements of a business plan. These should be helpful in writing any business plan, no matter who it's directed toward:

Make it easy to read. There is so much competition for investment dollars today, that if you want to get the jump on the next person, your plan will have to be well formatted and easily understood. Your introductory statement summarizing your operation is one of the most important sections—it must capture the investors' attention and motivate them to read the balance of the plan. If they need a dictionary at their side in order to read, they'll stop.

1.	Your approach should he market driven. Not product driven. If you want those magic doors to open you must understand that investors are primarily interested in how the product or service will react in the market. They want to see your research demonstrating how the customer will benefit before buying into your plan.

2.	Qualify the competition. Start by qualifying your product according to cost or time savings and revenue generation. Also show your projections for sales growth. And show how your product or service is superior to others, and how you intend to exploit the competitive advantage.

3.	Present your distribution plan. Be specific as to how the company will sell and distribute its product or service. Describe the method and what it will cost to get the product into the customer's hands.

4.	Exploit your company's uniqueness. Explain what will give your company a competitive edge in the marketplace—special attributes like patents, trade secrets, or copyrights.

5.	Emphasize management strength. Show proof that the company is comprised of highly qualified people who can cover all the bases. Indicate the incentives that will keep them together, and how they, the directors, and the advisers possess the necessary credibility.

6.	Present attractive projections. Paint a realistic picture of where your company is going from here. Be detailed and keep it credible. Good validated forecasts are impressive.

7. Zero in on possible funding sources. As mentioned earlier, it's different strokes for different folks.

Design versions of the plan to fit the idiosyncrasies of each source you plan to approach. A banker's interest lies in stability, security, and sound returns, whereas a venture capitalist is more interested in "early stage" funding, with higher risk and higher returns while a fund manager lay his eyes on the growth rate of the profit. All of them will want to know how much equity their investment will buy, and how the proceeds will be spent.

9. Close with a bang. Drive across the fact that you're offering a great deal. Be definite about how investors will get their money back and when. Specify the return: state how the investor will receive a 30 percent or 50 percent compounded annual return, or whatever you're offering.

## The Next Step

You're not finished yet. After you have drafted your business plan, solicit feedback on it. Ask a cross section of people in your business, whose judgment you trust, to review it. Don't fall in love with your words. Make the revisions that are necessary, then prepare a good oral presentation. In fact, you should have ready a two-minute and a five-minute oral attention grabber. Follow up with a detailed 15- to 30-minute presentation modeled on your written plan.

A word of caution: When preparing your financial projections, avoid the shortcut of relying on available computerized information—those preset formats in which you plug in figures and percentages. Individualize your financial projections. Think them out carefully. No two businesses are alike. And keep in mind that a new or start-up company won't fit the industry norm.

Your projections should include the financial obligations of bringing out your product: enlisting new management people and workers; taking on more space or manufacturing capacity; purchasing support materials; even the time it will take to receive your accounts receivables.

Expect to spend two or three months to write a business plan, with many more hours to prepare the presentation. Remember, your words not only have to paint a pretty picture, they must be persuasive as well.

It's of little use to approach the writing of a business plan as if it were a necessary evil. Rather look at it as a helpful tool that can be used to exploit the advantages of a product or service. There are many specifics that should be included in a successful business plan. The following outline contains many suggestions that may seem obvious, but one could easily forget to mention them. Again, this outline should be used as a preliminary planning guide.

## Business Plan Structure

1.      Cover sheet

Name, address, principal contact, phone, date.

2.      Table of contents

Categorize the contents.

3.      Executive summary

Very important. This summary briefly sets forth the contents, taking key sentences from each section of the plan to prepare the reader. Devote two or three pages to it.

4.      History

Include a brief description of how, when, and by whom the company was started, and its achievements, acceptance, setbacks, and current status.

5.      Product or Service

Describe the need for the product or service in today's marketplace, how it will make a difference, the benefits derived from using it, what will make the customer buy it, any other advantages or disadvantages. Explain any special training needed to sell or use it. Include all relevant regulation. Expound on any exclusivity or uniqueness.

6.   Market description and analysis

Prepare a customer profile. Describe what persons form your market, where they can be found, why they would purchase this product or service rather than another, and whether it would appeal to single individuals or to groups. Document quality, warranty, service, and price significance. Pinpoint the buyer and user. Point out political influences, if any. Describe market coverage, whether local, regional, national, or international.

Prepare an industry profile. Discuss pertinent trends, past, present, and future. Offer available statistical data on sales and units. Use charts, graphs, and tables if they seem impressive. Refer to trade associations if helpful.

Prepare a competitive profile. Stress advantages of price, quality, warranties, service, and distribution. Include the operational strengths and weaknesses. Project potential market share, trends in sales, and profitability.

Don't guess. Check your facts and note sources wherever possible.

7.   Marketing strategy

Specify the company's goals, how they are to be achieved, and who will have the responsibility. Qualify all distribution methods (representatives, dealers, and so forth) and describe any planned

advertising. Include sales aids, foreign licensing, and training.

8.   Operations plan

Disclose all present capabilities as to equipment and facilities, as well as future projections for offices, branches, manufacturing, and distribution.

9.      Research and development

Explain all past efforts and accomplishments as well as future expectations. Substantiate the patentability of inventions or other advantage the company will have over the competition, and the anticipated market impact.

10.     Schedule

Describe the timing and sequential steps that will be taken to bring the company up to full speed. Take it month by month for the first year. Thereafter, indicate the progress expected quarterly.

11.     Management

In the eyes of investors, the quality of the management team often determines the success of the company, so include detailed resumes. These should cover career highlights, accomplishments, positions heldf good performance records. Describe how the team has worked together in the past. List directors, consultants, advisers, and other key professionals who will be involved in company operations. Detailed resumes should be appended.

12.     Risks and problems

These could be a red flag. Indicate them only if the potential investor wants them identified.

13.     Use of proceeds

Judiciously present a timetable indicating how much money will be needed, when it will be needed, and how it will be used.

14.     Finances

Present the company's current equity capital structure as well as future plans. Itemize payments made with dates paid. List all outstanding stock options. Include profit and loss statements and balance sheets. Present current and proposed salary structure for those already on board and those who will come on board at a later date. Show projections month by month for the first year, quarterly for the second and third year's, and yearly thereafter.

15. Appendix

Include a glossary (if pertinent) and all essential pieces of evidence, such as resumes, product brochures, customer listings, testimonials, and news articles.

## Preprivate Financing

Information regarding preprivate and private financing prior to a public offering should also be included

in the business plan. To explain these terms: If two entrepreneurs each put up a certain amount of money to get a company started, that's preprivate financing. They then go out and seek more money—that's private financing from others. It's common practice and will not raise any eyebrows when presented in a good business plan.

## Special Executive Summary

This summary is not a part of the business plan; however, it takes advantage of the high points in the business plan. It serves as an entering wedge by the entrepreneur anticipating a public offering. It's called "special" because it stands alone.

The executive summary discussed earlier in the business plan outline usually summarizes the plan in two to three pages. The special executive summary expounds on the most enticing parts of the business plan for six to eight pages. In essence, it's a condensed business plan that shows a company to its best advantage. It's an entree when seeking help to locate and identify potential financial sources. It can also be used as an overview for persons who do not need to know all that much about the company, or for those from whom management wants to keep proprietary information. It can be changed and adapted to any particular audience. The special executive summary also serves as an informational document to create enthusiasm among brokers involved in selling the stock at the time of public offering. It certainly will make more interesting reading than a formal SEC document. A company should not go into an offering without it. Above all, a Special Executive Summary should not be taken lightly. It is indispensable, and should be kept updated. It could very well be a key to reaching the right money source.

## Follow-Up

A business plan requires regular updating. This should be given top priority. After a company has gone public and has raised the needed capital, the business plan should not be cast aside, but rather converted into an "operating plan." It should also be used to reflect on and to assist the management group in keeping the company focused on its goals. Refine it; adjust it; refer to it.

## Summary

If a company's goal is to go public, it must have a business plan. Preparing it may take months, but you won't make it to first base without it.

A company should give its plan its very best effort. You will discover that a well-prepared business plan will prove to be a vital sales tool when approaching any financial source, investor or lender.

A final note for anyone planning to go public: Failing to plan is planning to fail.

# Chapter 6

## THE MANAGEMENT TEAM -KEY TO SUCCEED

### The Management Team

In the game of hockey, the puck is passed from player to player until it is finally slammed towards the goal. In the game of business, it takes the same kind of teamwork to make a public company operate successfully. But as with any sport, it takes leadership to make the team work as a unit. This is management's role—to provide the vision, the direction, and the motivation to make the team a winner.

Let's take a look into the relationships, responsibilities, and qualities that can be expected from those members of the team in key management positions in a public company. These people are responsible for carrying out the directions of the CEO for the operation of the company. The CEO is the information and communications architect of the company, communicating to the team what must be done, while, by working together, they make it happen. Another responsibility of a public company's management team is to make certain that the company operates within the rules of the SEC. We all know that teams perform better when they're well motivated. In a public company, the motivation for management is usually the rewards of salary, stock options, and bonuses. These motivate individual players to play well, and ultimately makes the team perform well.

In today's business world, entrepreneur/CEOs are the primary creators of all new businesses. They were responsible for over 80 percent of new jobs created in the United States in the 1980s. The decade of the '80s was heralded by the financial press as the era of the entrepreneur.

The influence of the entrepreneur of the '80s is without parallel in our history. At the turn of this century, 80 percent of all Americans were self-employed. By 1950, this figure dropped to 18 percent. By 1970, just 20 years later, it dropped to just 9 percent. The 1980s saw a reverse in that trend as entrepreneurs moved to the forefront of a free enterprise-driven society. The results of their entrepreneurship and creativity have not only increased our quality of life, but caused revolutionary changes in our daily living.

Here are just a few examples of the impact made by entrepreneurs: Ray Kroc, the founder of McDonald's Corporation, was one of the prime contributors to the concept of fast foods in this country. His franchise operations opened the door to thousands of entrepreneurs who dreamed of self-employment and in the process expanded the job market. Mary Kay Ash, of Mary Kay Cosmetics, was responsible for millions of dollars being earned by second-income families, but more importantly, she helped thousands of women launch entrepreneurial lifestyles. The Block brothers, Henry and Richard, not only changed the practice of income tax preparation, but in the process built a $500 million company, and opened the door to thousands of new jobs. David Packard and William Hewlett created Hewlett-Packard. Today it's the largest manufacturer of electronic test and measurement equipment in the world. They trained and encouraged many people who now are among our most outstanding electronic entrepreneurs. And the list goes on.

In the past decade, thousands of entrepreneurs have created millions of jobs all over the world. Many thousands of new products and service ideas have been spawned in hundreds of industrial classifications. Few of these entrepreneurs could have accomplished their goals without the expertise of their management team.

While the value of a good management team is undeniable, deciding upon the right people to constitute a particular team can be a genuine challenge for CEOs. It requires careful evaluation of their own skills to determine the supplementary skills that will need to be provided by others on the management team.

The CEO's decision should be based on a thorough understanding of the business and what the members of the management team can bring with them to further that business. Their education and experience in business is essential to the company. It is also crucial for the entrepreneur/CEO to consider the personality of each team member, and his or her ability to deal with management problems that will be aired in public, to adapt to the frustrations and compromises involved in accomplishing short- or long-range goals, and to handle the continuing time diversions to accommodate public investors—let alone the burdensome reports constantly required by government agencies such as the SEC. In other words, besides having special abilities, the team members must be prepared to live in a goldfish bowl, even to the point of having their salary made public. These are only some of the factors that affect the important decisions an effective entrepreneur/CEO must make regarding the management team, but they are particularly important for building a strong team to run a public company.

The entrepreneur/CEO must understand, too, that the credentials and experience of the management team will be closely scrutinized by those involved in the investment process. Because, simply, that's what the game is all about!

Of course, the functions of the management team differ for different companies, depending on the nature of the company. For instance, some companies may require a research and development department, whereas a service company may not. An engineer-to-order manufacturing company and a fast food company require different kinds of management. Specific management abilities function in specific designated areas. Here I have prepared a general list of guidelines, qualifications, and fundamentals outlining abilities needed by members of the management team for a variety of public company environments:

## Administration and General Management

Planning. Ability to identify obstacles, establish attainable goals, develop and implement action plans

Problem Solving. Ability to gather and analyze facts, anticipate trouble and know what to avoid, implement solutions effectively and follow up thoroughly

Making Decisions. Ability to take input from the team and implement changes

Project and Task Management. Ability to properly define and set goals, organize participants, and monitor a project to completion

Negotiating. Ability to solicit differences from all sides, balance opinions, and fairly arbitrate for mutual benefit

Communication. Ability to communicate clearly and effectively to all parties and the public in both written and oral form

## Operations Management

Purchasing. Ability to seek out the most appropriate sources and suppliers, considering cost, delivery time, and quality; and to effectively negotiate contracts and manage flow, balancing current need and dollar resources

Manufacturing. Demonstrated experience in the process; open to continuous improvement techniques, people-power, machinery, time, costs, and quality needs of the customer

Inventory and Quality Control. Ability to establish suitable inspection standards, maintain accuracy, and set realistic dollar benchmarks for raw, in-process, and finished goods

## Financial Management

Ratios Applications. Ability to produce detailed pro formas for profit and loss (P&L), cash flow, and balance sheets; and analyze and monitor all financial areas

Money Controls. Ability to design, implement, and monitor all money management and to set up systems for overall and individual projects

Capital Raising. Ability to determine the best approach, form, structure debt/equity, short versus long term, and familiarity with sources

## Marketing Management

Evaluation and Research. Ability to conduct thorough studies using proper demographics and to

interpret and analyze the results in structuring viable territories and sales potential

Support. Ability to obtain market share by organizing, supervising, and most important, motivating a sales force

Planning. Ability to provide promotion, advertising, and sales programs that are effective with and for sales representatives and distributors

Selling. Ability to effectively demonstrate a capacity to identify, open the door, and develop new customers by closing the sale

Product Distribution. Ability to manage and supervise product flow from manufacturing through the channels of distribution to the end user, with attention to costs, scheduling, and planning techniques

Product Continuation. Ability to determine service and spare parts requirements, track customer complaints, supervise the setup and management of the service organization

## Engineering and R&D

Research. Ability to distinguish between basic and applied research, keeping a bottom-line balance Development. Ability to guide product development so that a product is introduced on time, within budget, and meets the customers' basic needs

Engineering. Ability to supervise the final design through engineering, testing, and manufacturing

## Personnel

Listening. Ability to listen without prejudging, really hear the message, and make effective decisions Help. Ability to determine situations where help is needed

Criticism. Ability to receive feedback without becoming defensive and to provide constructive criticism

Conflict. Ability to confront differences openly and determine resolution with teamwork

Development. Ability to select and coach subordinates and pass this ability on to peers

Culture. Ability to create an atmosphere and attitude conducive to high performance, rewarding work well done either verbally or monetarily

## Legal

Contracts. Experienced in and knowledgeable about the broad procedures and structure for government regulation and commercial law, including warranty, default, and incentives

Corporate. Experienced in and knowledgeable about the intricacies of incorporation, leases, distribution, stock issues, and patents

This list covers the qualifications, abilities, and characteristics the entrepreneur should take into account when assembling a management team for a public company.

A final word. It is not necessary to have the full team assembled and in place at the time of doing the reverse merger. In some cases, it is essential for the company to raise money upon the completion of the reverse merger. Here I would like to stress the importance to have a key person, in the case of Chinese company taking over an American shell, the key person is preferable to have an American background and working experiences. This will make a difference and might drives away some fear associated with the investment in the company.

## Summary

Choosing qualified, compatible people can be a long and laborious process, but the time is well spent if the end result spells success.

# Chapter 7

## CONSULTANTS AND ADVISORS

Too many cooks spoil the broth. That isn't necessarily so—especially when it comes to hiring consultants for small companies, or even large companies for that matter. No matter how professional a management team may be, and no matter how well staffed the company, there are usually areas of the business where it can use outside expertise. That's why consultants were born.

A consultant is a person with specialized expertise. Consultants are often retained on a onetime basis for a specific problem. Advisors, also discussed in this chapter, may also serve as consultants, but are expected to have a broader knowledge of the business. Advisors are usually retained to advise the company's management team for a longer term. They can be especially useful working through the reverse merger process.

### Consultants

Bringing in a consultant is not the same as hiring another person on the staff of the company. Consultants should be retained only for the period of time required to assist the management team in identifying, isolating, and solving problems or deficiencies. The consultant's function is to bring a particular problem into focus and zero in on the solution.

If there is a marketing problem, for example, the consultant may advise the company when to put a product on the market, whom the product should be directed to, and where the product is likely to receive a good reception. Or a consultant can provide expertise on product improvement or production techniques. There are countless situations where management could be served by help from a professional on the outside.

## Consultants Can Come from Anywhere

Anyone can call himself or herself a consultant. Some people who call themselves consultants are self-promoters. Some work at it on a temporary basis. They are often people with good management skills who are between jobs, or they can be former CEOs who offer expertise in their particular fields.

## Hire When Ready!

When enlisting the aid of a consultant or consulting firm, the company should first be convinced of the need. According to a recent Harvard Business Review article, "Management consultants are generally hired for the wrong reasons. Once hired, they are generally poorly employed and loosely supervised."

Therefore it is important that the company does its homework before hiring a consultant. Most consultants have an area of specialty. Some may claim broad expertise, but their experience may actually He in a special industry or technical area. The company should find out this information in advance. The fact that a consultant has an excellent background in one field does not make him or her an expert in another field. The company should also determine in advance the precise problem needing a solution—thus eliminating some consultants from the running.

## Consultants Are Not Always Necessary

Properly utilized, a consultant can appreciably help a company's operations, but too often management may already have the answer to a problem, and only need to convince key people. The consultant can serve that purpose, but at a price. Consultants also are often asked to explore areas the company has no intention of pursuing. Yet another misuse of company money is to hire consultants to research information that is readily available.

A sharp management group can solve many consulting chores without paying unnecessary consulting fees. For instance, suppliers can usually advise a company whether it is more advantageous to buy or lease certain assets, or how best to go about computerizing a business with the right kind of hardware and software. Insurance company agents are trained to determine the most efficient insurance and employee benefit plans. Advertising agencies and marketing companies interested in working with the company will usually provide sound, useful information for free. All it takes is a little talking to the people a company does business with or plans to do business with. Remember, a consultant is not the only one who can supply answers.

Consultant is not a magic word. Consultants should not be left to their own devices. Management has an obligation to stay on top of consultants activities as well as to make certain they get the necessary support from the company's staff Consultants should be encouraged to bring in solutions within a reasonable period of time. As mentioned in an earlier chapter: Time is Money.

## Fees

Consulting fees can take many forms. They are often open to negotiation, but some consultants are firm in their charges. Much depends on the complexities involved. Fees can be based on hourly time or a weekly amount. Some consultants ask for a fixed fee or retainer. Some companies prefer to have consultants work in-house, but some consultants will work only off site.

The ideal way for the company to approach the consultant situation would be to contact several possible consultants. Brief them on the problem. Secure proof of their expertise and information on similar projects they have worked on. Besides asking for

44

their credentials and resume, request specific proposals on how the project could be handled.

Before the final decision is reached, management should feel confident of working with the consultant and satisfied of receiving:

1. A realistic and reasonable charge for services

2. A determined attempt to produce results

3. A cooperative attitude toward the people involved

4. Maintenance of a continuing relationship

The effort and time involved in securing the services of the right consultant for a particular need will pay off handsomely. The chemistry must be there, for with it comes the confidence and security the job will be done right.

## Advisors

Don't even think about going public without the backing of knowledgeable advisors. There are more obstacles to be encountered in the reverse merger process than in the game of Monopoly, from finding the right shell to resume listing on the OTC.BB.

The best advisors—the most dependable advisors—are those persons or consulting firms that have been through the reverse merger battle from beginning to end more than once. You may have to search,

because there are not very many of them out there, but they are the only sure way to go. What's more, even though the advisors may have been through the process, they'll find it different every time. The rules change from day to day with the never-ending changes in federal and state regulations and the fickleness of the financial community, which wants every speculative investment to be a sure thing.

Other advisors not specifically covered in the study, but who should be considered even more important, are people who have been through the reverse merger process and who could apply their knowledge and experience for the benefit of the company-people such as a member of the board of directors or someone in the management team who has been involved in the reverse merger process before, or an experienced outside investment banker with prior dealings with reverse mergers. What matters is having a broad perspective of the process and being objective about what the CEO must contend with in confrontations with other professionals, such as attorneys, CPAs, and the SEC and other governmental agencies.

This was not surprising, as lawyers play a key role in almost every aspect of a company going public. It's especially advantageous to have legal counsel with a strong working knowledge of the reverse merger process.

CPAs who have been through the process can be invaluable in showing the company to its best advantage. The end result of any business has to do with accountability—profit and loss. CPAs with a working knowledge of reverse merger can evaluate how well the company's earning stream will hold up. They can put the company in touch with the shell company as well as the fund mangers. They can also act as a bridge between the CEO and the SEC legal department and advise the entrepreneur whether the company can be competitive in the market.

Printers' contributions to a listing on OTC.BB can be critical, for they are involved in the process from beginning to end. On their shoulders fall the supervision of the preparation and issuance of documents, including the prospectus and registration statement, which must be flawless. A small spelling mistake could ruin the whole thing. Also, the printing of all the documents can be very costly. As an advisor, the printer can help the company obtain quality work at the best price.

## Summary

Entrepreneur/CEOs contemplating a reverse merger are well advised to surround themselves with experienced, professional, outside people. While there are many highly qualified consultants and advisors who have been through the process and can advise on all phases, not just anyone with the title of consultant or advisor will suffice. All persons can't be all things to all companies. If an operation is for chest surgery, it would be ridiculous to ask an dentist to do the job. It's imperative to seek out people with expertise in the company's specialty. It also helps if the experts have a cooperative attitude and contacts in the financial community.

For a company going public, the right consultants and advisors can help a company make history rather than become history.

# Chapter 8

## ACCOUNTANTS AND REGULATION S-X ACCOUNTING

One of the key figures in a company going public is the accountant. If the books aren't in order, if the figures don't check and balance, the company doesn't stand a chance of satisfying the SEC requirements for public companies. Therefore, the roie of the accountant is most crucial to the completion of any reverse merger case.

### Selecting Accountants

According to law, every public company must have audited financial statements. Not only that, but when going public, the company must have an SEC-qualified accountant perform the audit. To be considered qualified, the accountant or accounting firm must be a member of the SEC Practice Section of the American Institute of CPAs (certified public accountants).

Since, by law, every business has to prepare financial statements, sophisticated entrepreneurs seek out the services of a certified public accountant (CPA) to prepare the different required reports.

### Compilations

A compilation is the simplest of the CPA reports, generally performed for internal company use only. The purpose is to give the accountant a general understanding of the nature of the company's business, the accounting records, and company policies. The CPA reads the company's financial statements and makes sure they are in appropriate form and free from clerical errors. The figures are supplied by management, and the CPA does not express any opinion about them.

## Reviews

A review is a report that goes beyond the compilation. It provides some assurance about the reliability of the financial statements. The company accountant or CPA reviews the accounting principles and practices of the company and its industry, and analyzes and compares expected trends, past results, industry data, and internal projections. The review may also contain some of the specific procedures that would ordinarily be performed in an audit.

## Audits

An audit is a confirmation of the credibility and reliability of the financial statement of a company. Every IPO and public company has to have an audited financial statement performed by an outside audit accountant (CPA) to guard against company manipulations in the report. The accountant reviews and evaluates the effectiveness of all the accounting procedures and internal controls that are necessary to meet SEC accounting standards for public companies. The accountant must also attest to the correctness of the company's financial statements and to the company's financial position for the period covered.

It is the responsibility of an existing company going public to present the auditing accountant with as complete and correct financial records as possible to verify the income statements. If the balance sheets and inventory verification are not possible to reconstruct, a cloud on the audit could result: a "qualified" financial opinion on the part of the audit accountant that could delay the offering by the SEC until a full year of auditable inventory has taken place.

## Preparation

It bears repeating: Companies in the early stages of doing business should make preparations for the eventuality of going public. They should start by assembling an accounting team. The team should consist of inside (often called in-house), outside (usually a CPA), and audit accountants.

An in-house accountant should have bookkeeping and accounting experience, but need not be a full-fledged accountant. The position includes responsibility for day-to-day routine bookkeeping functions and coordinating with the outside accountant. As the company grows, there may be an increasing need to bring in a full-fledged accountant.

The outside accountant is independent, not personally involved with the company, and preferably a CPA. It's important that the CEO has respect and confidence in this person, who represents a link between the company and the SEC accounting world. This accountant usually prepares or at least reviews the monthly financial statements and supervises the assembly of the company's quarterly and annual reports. The position requires someone familiar with and knowledgeable in SEC accounting procedures, as well as being able to serve as liaison between the company and audit accountants.

## Audit Accounting

Audit accounting is a subject warranting a closer look. Auditing accountants must be completely independent. They must not have any financial interest or ownership in the company. SEC auditing accountants work in teams. Their job is to look for trouble in the books, so they tend to be suspicious. They seem to trust no one, especially no one in the company. They can be expected to check and cross-check every item. That's what they're paid to do.

## Audit Guidelines

SEC Regulation S-X deals with the form and content of financial statements and their ultimate certification. It spells out the importance of independent auditing accountants and details the rules and regulations that must be adhered to by audit accountants in order to establish their independence. It further sets out qualifications to guarantee that independence, including:

* Independence during the full period of audit
* No financial interest in the company
* Cannot be a promoter, officer, director, or employee of the company
* Cannot certify another auditor's work
* Must avoid interrelations with employees or relatives of employees of the company
* Must perform the audit personally, without subcontracting it to others
* Cannot "write up the books" (post the general ledger) a function that must be done by in-house accountant)

Also, SEC rules state that the company cannot owe the independent auditor for past audit fees.

SEC Regulation S-X seems to infringe upon the auditor's basic rights in making any contact with management or employees strictly taboo. However, the SEC looks upon these rules as a way to assure the independence of the auditor and to make certain that favoritism in any form towards the company does not take place.

## Qualifying the Auditing Accountant

There are many ways to qualify an auditing firm. One way is to get recommendations from a trusted person, someone knowledgeable about the reverse merger process, or from the company's reverse merger advisor or attorney. Although heavy SEC experience is not critical for the accounting firm, since set guidelines are followed by all accountants, it is nonetheless essential that the firm have some experience in SEC accounting. For an reverse merger, you shouldn't make a move without an audit accountant who has been through the registration process more than once--and recently! Any CPA firm can work the numbers game, but not all CPA firms can play the SEC numbers game to the benefit of the client. Also important to remember, the managing partner in the accounting firm should be the sign-off person, as someone fully accountable for the detail work of subordinates.

Another good way to qualify an auditing firm is by interview. Select several promising contenders and request proposals for final evaluation. Ask questions such as:

* What are the firm's areas of expertise?
* What is its recent SEC filing experience?
* Who will work with the company day to day?
* What are the billing methods? By hour? By job?
* What is the billing cycle?
* When can someone begin?
* How long will it take?
* Does the firm have underwriter or investor contacts?
* Will it give an estimated total cost in a written proposal?

## Familiarity Is a Must

Every effort should be made to hire audit accountants familiar with the company's type of business and industry. It is also beneficial if they have experience with competitors—as long as their other client is not presently in direct competition with your company.

Familiarity helps because audit requirements differ vastly from industry to industry. For example, an oil pipe supply company's inventory occupies many acres of outdoor storage whereas the inventory of a fast food franchise is turned over by being eaten every day, and a manufacturer of high-tech small parts may fit three months' inventory in a few fireproof file drawers. Bookkeeping, payable, and receivable methods vary from company to company. This results in special rules being applied to different types of companies and to their various stages of development. The auditing accountant must have the skill and knowledge to work through these differences. That is why familiarity can be a plus.

Actually, audit accountants are bound by an ethical code to turn down companies that may represent a potential conflict of interest. Nevertheless, a base familiarity with the company's business should be considered very valuable indeed.

## GAAP Must Be Observed

GAAP is an industry term. It means Generally Accepted Accounting Principles. GAAP dictates the principles for presenting audit information. As an example, accounting methods of private companies are generally aimed toward decreasing taxable income and depreciation. Inventory booking and write-downs are adjusted accordingly. Private companies frequently switch back and forth from cash to accrual accounting methods to assist in tax adjustment. These practices are not allowed for public companies that function under GAAP. All accounting for public companies must be done on an accrual basis.

In a case where an existing company has operating subsidiaries, the subsidiaries must also have financials audited under GAAP. This makes for auditing headaches, especially if offshore subsidiaries are involved. Separate audits must also be prepared for subsidiaries that may be sole proprietors or partnerships.

Although the process of auditing an existing company that has not previously been audited can be costly and time consuming, it can be done, providing the company has maintained fairly complete financial records. However, getting into the area of Inventory may be a different matter.

Inventory verification, within GAAP, can become very complicated. It must include historical (prior) audited financials, which can present a sticky problem for the auditor who was not around when the inventory items were first counted. Consequently, many companies may find themselves in the awkward position of writing off large amounts of inventory with the audit opinion qualified regarding past inventory procedures. In essence, the auditor says, "Since I wasn't involved in taking the inventory count, I can't truly say that all the statements are absolutely correct. But I assume they are."

For inventory accounting, the auditor must know whether the inventory valuation has been applied on a consistent basis—was the method used last in first out (LIFO) or first in first out (FIFO)?—as there is often a price variation in the interim. What, if any, tax adjustments were made and how they affected the tax reporting are other possible variables, as well as the inclusion of overhead in finished goods inventory, a requirement of the SEC. And, of course, the method used for inventory accounting must be acceptable to GAAP.

Prior to the new SEC regulations, the audit accountant could simply state in effect, "I was not present to physically observe the taking of the prior year's inventory; however, I did physically monitor the most recent inventory. Consequently, it is my opinion that all past inventories were properly conducted, and I believe all accounts are reasonable." Because this type of statement occasionally proved to be incorrect, the SEC has disallowed the practice, and now insists on a clean, fully satisfied "I did physically observe all inventory."

## Time Costs Money

A forward-looking entrepreneur/CEO with the goal of eventually taking the company public should seriously consider enlisting the services of an accountant to monitor and audit inventory procedures from the start. The cost will be considerably less than a fully audited financial statement, and so will the aggravation. It won't eliminate the necessity of an audit when going public, but it will save time and dollars, even if a different accounting firm becomes involved with the reverse merger. What's more, even if a company's inventory has been audited regularly, prior audits must be reviewed to assure compliance with SEC regulations.

An audit for a small existing company can take from a few weeks to possibly one month. It depends on the problems the auditing accountant may uncover. Previously unaudited companies are typically beset with such deficiencies as poor accounts payable systems, uncollectible accounts receivable that haven't been written off or down, unreconciled bank accounts, notes payable with doubled assets pledged as underlying collateral, and incorrectly recorded depreciation expenses.

Accounting ethics require strict adherence to due diligence procedures. For instance, if the company purchased a major piece of equipment, the accountants will have to see copies of purchase orders, invoices, and canceled checks. They will be expected to inquire about possible securities fraud violations and bankruptcy filings.

Areas that can present very complicated problems for previously unaudited existing companies include personal financial dealings by officers and directors that were placed through the corporation. Even advances or loans made to officers by the company, especially in recent accounting periods, require special schedules to be filled out and reported.

All of the these issues take time to resolve, and the cost varies according to the time involved. It's not unusual for an auditing firm to charge as much as $200,000 for a reverse merger case.

## Audit Accountants Are Accountable

Audit accountants today must take full responsibility for their work. SEC CPAs can be held liable for misleading or false financial data in a prospectus. If they were misled by company falsification but cannot establish that they conducted their work with sufficient diligence, they are accountable under the Securities Act of 1933 through the comfort letter we spoke about in an earlier chapter. This leaves them vulnerable to lawsuits by both the SEC and investors.

Experienced auditors know that the financial statements they submit will be used in the prospectus of a company going public. They know that the prospectus basically serves as a selling document. Therefore, they can be expected to make every effort to express their findings in clear, concise, and easily understood language, down to the thoroughness of the footnotes in the financials. Their reputation rides on the effectiveness of their presentation. And so does their next job.

## Summary

A company anticipating a reverse merger should make every effort to create a good working relationship with an SEC-qualified and knowledgeable accounting firm, preferably one versed in the reverse merger process. It's also advantageous if the accountant is familiar with the company's business and can efficiently perform all the required SEC accounting procedures for that particular company. The right firm will provide continuing counsel and guidance as well as assist the company in all its financial statements and proceedings that require SEC approval. It would be especially desirable

for the accounting firm to have working contacts with SEC legal counsel, and investment banking firms. When it comes to selecting an accounting firm for a company going public, it should not only be what you know, but who you know.

Today's regulatory environment requires an opinioned audit from an accredited accounting firm. It is therefore important that the management of the company going public understand completely the specific rules that apply for public company operations. Most important is that their audit accountant remain independent of all company involvement.

# Chapter 9

## ATTORNEYS

### ATTORNEYS

Highly specialized. Past REVERSE MERGER experience. Compatible, intelligent, knowledgeable. Friendly, if possible. Good contacts with underwriters, investors, bankers, and brokers. Reasonable fee.

Well, the last may be asking too much. But that's the kind of counsel that makes a reverse merger a happy experience. The company must depend on legal counsel to see it through compliance with a multitude of federal and state securities laws and regulations. If all is not done according to SEC rules, which require a keen legal mind to decipher, the reverse merger can be stopped in its tracks.

### Letting Go

Unfortunately, it's not easy to let go of the friendly legal counsel who has seen a company through thick and thin. However, as private companies grow, and contemplate going public, they must be prepared to make changes—unless their present or regular attorney has SEC experience. Most competent attorneys will realize their limitations and even suggest bringing in a highly competent, recognized specialist in the reverse merger process.

Every effort should be made to select counsel with reverse merger experience in an industry similar to yours. Although many legal firms have an active SEC practice, their experience may have been in dissimilar industries, and their involvement may be limited to ongoing companies, as opposed to new filings.

Some attorneys specialize in oil and gas, or gold mining filings; others have expertise in high-tech filings. Large, prestigious law firms are usually geared to handle more complicated SEC filings, whereas smaller law firms may not be. The secret is to select an attorney or firm familiar with the business of the company going public and, we emphasize, experienced in reverse merger filings.

## The Difference Between Large and Small

Like shoes, legal firms come in different sizes and styles. Many of them specialize in various types of services. It's up to company management to choose the firm that best fits the company's requirements as to size, compatibility, competency, and contacts in the investment community.

A large legal firm is not the answer for all companies. True, a large firm may have several hundred lawyers with many areas of specialties. On the surface that may seem advantageous. Many large corporations prefer such firms, as they can call upon the services of different specialists in one office. That arrangement may serve the purpose of a diversified, multidimensional company with many different companies under one umbrella—say a manufacturing company, a mining company, a food company, and a service company—each requiring different legal input. A small reverse merger case lacking that corporate makeup wouldn't need a firm with all those attorneys whereby it may face the possibility of getting lost in the shuffle.

Large legal firms with many partners and associates traditionally also have many young, inexperienced junior associate attorneys. These are usually assigned to work with small companies on a day-to-day basis. Since the associates must often clear their advice with a managing partner, dealings can become frustrating for the company management as well as inefficient, time consuming, and costly. Those new, bright, young lawyers, although capable and intelligent, lack experience, and they can make a lot of mistakes. It's a learning process for them, but it's usually the client who pays for their mistakes.

Depending on the benefits and prestige derived from engaging a large law firm versus a small firm, it may be preferable for a reverse merger to work with a small, SEC-specialized legal firm. For one thing, the company will get closer attention. Junior associates or paralegals become involved usually only to help out in routine matters. Small firms can be fully competent to handle all the corporate information, including all the SEC rules and regulations. Specializing in companies going public, they are usually more cognizant of the nuances of prospectus writing and more aware of the current SEC environment; that's their whole business.

## Getting Along

Too often the attorney's image is that of a necessary evil. Attorneys have been typecast as arrogant, nonresponsive, and overpriced. In fact, some are really nice. But rarely do they come cheap. However, in the eyes of reasonable entrepreneurs, the price is right if it gets them through the reverse merger.

## Setting Parameters

It's up to management to set the parameters when selecting counsel for a reverse merger case. Management should be clear about what it expects—whether it's hand holding, assurances that the company's goals to go public are attainable, or even alternatives on how the reverse merger can best be achieved. Management must also cooperate fully with counsel. It's the attorney's responsibility to write a full disclosure document describing the company, its markets, the competition in the market, and its product or services.

There must be no secrets kept from counsel. The more the counsel understands the company's industry, its management team, and its aspirations, the more helpful he or she can be, and less frustrated. Forthrightness will also save time, which translates directly into dollars.

## Questions to Ask

When interviewing for reverse merger counsel, it's advisable for management to prepare a list of questions for a potential law firm or attorney to answer to assist the CEO in the selection process. The following questions can prove helpful in making the decision:

* What types of registration has your firm worked with in the past?

* Do you have recent filing experience?

* Do you have particular areas of business specialty, and are they compatible with our company's industry?

* Who will be our day-to-day contact?

* What is your billing procedure? Hourly, or monthly, or by segments?

* Can you give us your estimated total cost, including expenses and fees?

* Do you have any useful investment contacts? Underwriters, brokers, investors?

* What is your projected timetable? How long do you expect the process to take?

* When will you be able to start on the project?

## Billing and Fees

Reverse merger attorneys typically bill by time and they count not just hours, but minutes. Their rationalization is that they do not sell products or services; they sell knowledge and past experience, which can be invaluable to a client.

Although hourly rates can vary from less than a hundred dollars to several hundred, a good round figure for the primary senior contact member of a law firm would be about $150 per hour. Time for junior associates could be in the area of $75 an hour, and administrative functions (typing, copying) could range from $30 to $50 per hour. These are give and take figures.

Total fees can vary considerably. A simple reverse merger charger could be in the range of $15,000 to $20,000. The more complex process for the shell company with past history is usually more costly. It requires going back into the company's past and reviewing the minutes, article and bylaw changes, patents, employment, license agreements, financing, and clarification of anything that may put a cloud on the company's operations.

Ethical law firms usually provide an estimate of the total costs. It's a safe guess that the final amount will seldom be less than the estimate. Although some firms are willing to put a cap on the project, they will usually leave an out for themselves for unanticipated exigencies. These could be article or bylaw changes, unexpected litigation, state law changes, unresolved lawsuits, or new SEC requirements. The entrepreneur can make book there will be something.

It is also unrealistic to assume that legal counsel will work on the contingency that the fee will be paid after the reverse merger is completed, regardless of the negotiated amount. It's best to plan on a deposit or advance. A reasonable figure would be a percentage of the total estimated fee, or an estimate of the first month's work or of the first stage of work. Rarely will any substantial work be performed by a reverse merger law firm prior to an initial payment, usually made at the time of signing an engagement letter.

## Other Forms of Payment

Generally speaking, the legal profession is not averse to taking a flyer with the company. Many attorneys like reverse megers, not only because they generate handsome fees, but because they like the idea of taking a portion of their fees in stock. The structure of the legal business in itself does not generate capital appreciation or equity buildup. Consequently, accepting stock as part payment allows lawyers to become more intimately involved with the company and gives them an opportunity to invest without actually putting out any hard cash.

Paying stock in lieu of money can create problems. For one thing, it can dilute ownership among stockholders in the company. It can cause disagreement among the

61

partners in the law firm, too. Especially in larger firms, it often happens that partners who are not directly involved in the project may not feel as positive about the company's potential. They would prefer the cash to restricted stock that has no guarantees.

The strongest argument against stock as payment is the potential conflict of interest. Some company managers may question whether the advice they are receiving is in their interest or the advisor's interest. Attorneys in the law firm may question a conflict of interest regarding the involvement of outside parties and whether it would be condoned by the SEC. The ability to remain objective when negotiating non-arm's-length transactions may also be questioned. These may seem extreme concerns, but should not be ignored in a decision whether to offer stock for the services of legal counsel.

## Double-Check the Cost

As mentioned earlier, the cost of doing business with a reverse merger law firm is high under the best of circumstances. Therefore, it's just common sense to make a practice of regularly reviewing counsel's billings. To err is forgivable. Not to check the error can be expensive. Time and again, good relationships between management and legal counsel have dissolved because it seemed counsel was taking advantage regarding billings. This assumption, more often than not, turns out to be unfounded. But that is why professional legal counsel is always ready to discuss, substantiate, and if necessary, adjust billings. It's up to the company to keep the lines of communication open and frank. Establishing a good working relationship is of benefit to both company and counsel.

## Legal Responsibilities

The role and responsibilities of legal counsel are covered more fully in subsequent chapters involving:

* Pre-reverse merger planning
* Corporate record cleanup

* Review of all contracts and agreements

* Amending articles and bylaws

* Capital structure

Other areas that involve legal counsel are preparing information for the SEC, advising on exemptions and their impact on the company, and developing stock incentive plans that meet SEC regulations. These are all part of the process of making the company ready to go public that leads up to the actual presentation of the registration statement and the filing.

Judicial decisions have played havoc with the accounting profession, resulting in accounting firms being named in shareholder lawsuits. Accountants were the first to be blamed for "improper" company financial records. Judges soon discovered complicity on the part of the legal profession, which increasingly became named in these suits after companies faltered. Today, accountants and attorneys, as well as management and directors are jointly sued by disgruntled shareholders. As a result, the fees of all continue to rise.

## The Multiple Counsel Approach

It is common practice today for entrepreneurs going public to continue the employment of lawyers they worked with in the past or are currently working with. Existing companies frequently remain with the corporate counsel they have felt comfortable with, even lacking SEC experience. They may also use outside counsel in areas such as patent, trademark, copyright, real estate, or other specialties. The SEC attorney is another specialist who will supervise the reverse merger undertaking. Working with the company's corporate attorney should present no problem, but rather be of help in general business issues.

Retaining the company attorney could very well save the company hefty legal fees. For many items, instead of paying the high hourly rate of the SEC counsel, the company can pay its regular counsel, usually at a much lower rate, to clean up and update company records needed in the reverse merger process. The two lawyers can complement each other as well as realize a savings for the company. In the final analysis, it's a "save and sound" idea.

## Summary

For small reverse mergers, small legal firms or individual attorneys with SEC expertise are often preferable to large legal firms. Of course, it depends on how complex and involved the reverse merger is. Choosing counsel should never be approached as a crapshoot by management, as SEC attorneys play a major role in the final resolution of a public offering.

Personal compatibility is a paramount consideration. The relationship of management and counsel is often likened to a marriage, as they will be practically living together during the reverse merger time period. Legal costs for a highly qualified SEC counsel also need continuing evaluation. These costs can be the second largest item in an underwriting, but cost should never be the overriding factor in the selection of an attorney. More important is current and repeated experience in filings, and familiarity with the company's business is especially helpful. Remember, it is the responsibility of legal counsel to make sure the company going public complies with the federal and state securities laws.

Payment in stock for legal services, although seemingly inviting, should be carefully considered, as it may lead to long-term complications. But it can be reassuring to know that SEC attorneys are human. They're not ogres or gougers, and their success with a reverse merger means better recommendations and more jobs for them. Remember, they want that golden ring as badly as the company does.

# Chapter 10

## FINANCIAL PRINTERS

## FINANCIAL PRINTERS

Financial printers are a breed unto themselves. They are specialists in the printing of financial documents, including registration statements, prospectuses, even stock certificates. On the surface this may sound like nothing out of the ordinary. Not so. It calls for complete involvement with the client.

The documents cannot be distributed if they are not letter perfect. There can be no typos or errors. After proofreading by all key parties, the printer will make an additional review to make sure all necessary elements are included and correct before going to press. No one concerned can consider these to be run-of-the-mill printing jobs.

Not just any printer can do financial printing. Recognized financial printers must stay current with the strict SEC rules, regulations and printing requirements regarding size of type and paper, format, and other technical specifications. Nothing short of 100 percent accuracy is acceptable.

To expedite the printing, management needs to assure that each proof is promptly reviewed by all the key parties. It is usual for management to authorize one person to communicate and coordinate the project with the printer. Many companies rely on SEC counsel to handle that chore. Another time-saver is to assign one person, a secretary or the central editor to submit corrected copy to the printer with all the correct spelling, punctuation, and content. It will avoid a lot of confusion and allow the printer to move fast.

You need 100 percent cooperation, dedication to the job, and know-how from the printer, probably explaining why there are only about 20 qualified financial printers in the United States today. (Lists are available through most brokerage houses and underwriters.)

Confidentiality is another reason for using experienced, qualified financial printers. They are well aware of the importance of keeping inside information from leaking. They are accustomed to working behind a veil of secrecy and know the implications. They know that companies they work for must be able to trust them and feel comfortable with their security precautions.

## Costs

Financial printing is not cheap. As of this writing, it can cost you 30,000 dollars.

## Qualifying the Financial Printer

The company's attorney usually has the best access to qualified financial printers. Recommendations can also come from the reverse merger advisor, the underwriter, and the financial public relations firm. Because the outlay for financial printing is substantial, a wise management team will ask for several recommendations. There are not that many printers to choose from, but it's important to find the one that can offer the best deal as to price and performance. Printers with computerized equipment are capable of accepting floppy disks and other word-processing input directly from the attorney's office, saving time and money.

Here are some pertinent questions a company should ask a potential financial printer:

1.      Could we have a list of your recent clients?

2.      What type of facilities do you operate?

3.      May we have samples of recent similar jobs?

4. How long have you done financial printing?

5. Do you expect computer, hard copy, or both from us?

6. Can you give us an estimate of the cost of the complete job, breaking out any extras?

7. Who will be your contact person?

Management should carefully evaluate the responses to select a printer who will fulfill the company's requirements and with whom company personnel can work comfortably.

## Ancillary Services

Stock certificates are also printed by financial printers, though no longer exclusively. Few public companies any longer use the elaborately engraved certificates of earlier days, but now choose preprinted certificates, simply inserting the company name and logo for a customized look.

Most financial printers also provide full conference room facilities, complete with bar and kitchen, to offer clients comfortable surroundings where they can proof their documents and make last-minute changes before going to press.

Financial printers are also geared for handling the distribution of both preliminary and final prospectus to broker/dealers, and other members of the financial community. The printer will sort and deliver copies to the various places and people specified by the lead underwriter—the service isn't free, but it relieves the company from a burdensome task.

## Summary

Financial printing is a specialized field. Only about 20 firms throughout the United States can meet SEC standards in printing the documents required by a company going public, from the registration statement to the prospectus. They will cost you money, but you should get your money's worth in a printer who will remain involved in the distribution of the documents, working closely with the management of a reverse merger; and confidentiality is part of the job.

Although there are few financial printers to choose from, they are competitive. It pays to shop for one that fits your budget, delivers the product on time, and most important, guarantees accuracy.

Remember, if it's worth doing at all—it had better be done right!

# Chapter 11

## FINANCIAL PUBLIC RELATIONS

Financial public relations, as it pertains to public companies traded over the counter, and especially to small ones, is usually sadly lacking. The reason is that, unfortunately, management of too many small companies just don't comprehend the value of financial public relations. In fact, it's often a totally foreign subject to them. They don't understand how important it is to get out information about the company to brokers to keep them hyped up, to members of the public so that they will buy the stock, to shareholders to keep them from selling their stock, and to the media generally. Too few people in management think "Out of sight, out of mind" could possibly pertain to their company.

A wise entrepreneur knows, "You gotta sell the company to sell the company." entrepreneurs astute enough to include financial public relations in their business program, even on a limited basis, stand a greater chance of success than those who neglect it.

### The Public Relations Mystique

There's really no mystery about public relations except perhaps in the minds of some members of management teams. Financial public relations is simply a means of informing the public what a company is doing, in such a way as to make the public take notice and take the kind of action that enables the company's goals to be reached—that is, buy the company's stock.

Public relations begins within the company in the day-to-day conduct of business. It's the shine on a salesperson's shoes, the smile on a face, a friendly greeting. A welcome attitude by a receptionist. A telephone call put through promptly by a telephone operator. It's a cordial letter by the company president. It's employees who think and speak well of the company. Public relations is, in essence, a state of mind with a positive attitude toward anyone who hears about, reads about, or comes in contact with the company.

## Four Steps to effective Corporate Financial Public Relations

Embarking on a financial public relations program can be divided into four basic steps:

1.        Analysis: PR people will first analyze the public's attitude toward the company: Is it positive? Negative? Indifferent? They may resort to a public opinion poll or an attitude survey. They may randomly ask people what kind of feelings they have toward the company or industry. Or the PR people may have enough research on hand to proceed with the next step.

2.        Interpretation and Policy Making: After an understanding of public opinion regarding the company has been gained through formal or informal means, the next step is evaluating these opinions in order to formulate policies and objectives. Then PR must prepare plans to achieve these objectives.

Effective corporate financial public relations revolves around this interpretation, planning, and decision-making. Plans should cover existing conditions—products, markets, sales performance (if significant), competition, policies, dealers and distributors, and the various people the company wishes to reach. The objective is always to create an interest in the company as one that should be invested in. Specific needs and goals must be set forth to reach this objective. Methods include human interest stories, news releases, or other forms of communication such as broadcasting,

TV, or printed material. They should take into consideration the results of research, including attitudes and public opinion. The goal is to reach all interested parties—shareholders, investors, underwriters, and the financial press.

3. Communication: The basic message to be communicated should be established and agreed upon. The target audience should be clearly defined in order to reach the greatest possible number of the persons whom the message is aimed at. Appropriate media should be used, whether brochures, newsletters, newspapers, even broadcasting. The more people who can become interested in the company, the greater potential there is of the stock going up in value.

4. Continuing Evaluation: PR should not be considered a one-time effort. The results of programs and the effectiveness of techniques should be constantly evaluated. Although the corporation may have gained approval today, there is no assurance it will continue through tomorrow. Attitudes and opinions of individuals change with time, with new points of view, and information from competing sources.

Markets also change. New markets develop. Income levels and populations shift, changes which may necessitate company diversification. Technology may change. The need for venture capital may arise. All of these factors require a company to be prepared to alter its strategy. It will pay off in increased profits and future growth for a company to constantly reevaluate its public relations program.

To reiterate: A financial public relations program begins with building a favorable image and a friendly climate of opinion in which to operate. Maintaining them is critical to a company's success. It stands to reason, if a company is perceived to have growth potential, chances are it will have more stock buyers.

## The Public Relations Difference

There is a difference between financial and other public relations. In "other," the company is mainly concerned with its community image, its customers, its suppliers, its employees, and its standing in the industry. In financial public relations, there is a focus on those areas that affect the public's impression of the company financially. Of key concern are existing and prospective shareholders. The goal is to attract new shareholders while retaining the old ones, because the more a company has of both, the greater chance its stock has of going up in value.

The CEO of a company is rarely involved in the sale of its stock. Sales are usually handled by market-maker contacts, printed material, news releases, and the efforts of financial public relations.

## The Rewards of Financial PR

in most companies, the CEO or a key member of the management team will have the responsibility for implementing and overseeing the financial public relations program, making it even more important that they have an awareness of all the areas financial PR encompasses. It's through financial public relations that management is able to maximize the company's progress and development, not only for itself, but for all shareholders.

Also to be considered is that with the increase of the trading price of the company's stock, management's personal net worth increases, which naturally makes for a more contented management.

All starts with the fact that any stock on any exchange or market faces a potential demand every day it's traded—and that demand usually originates in the concerted efforts of financial public relations. Stocks go up when there are more buyers than sellers. Stocks go down when there are more sellers than buyers. If a company is perceived to have growth potential, chances are that it will have more buyers. It's the job of the financial PR firm to let the public know that the company is there and that good things are happening to it.

Unfortunately, a common cry among financial PR people is that many corporations think of them only as a means to put out fires, and too often the PR people have good reason for complaint. But hiring a qualified financial public relations firm is one of the best investments an IPO can make. PR can set the fires that a reverse merger needs to gain the recognition and acceptance that it seeks.

Today's investors are more sophisticated. With new stock disclosure laws, there is less manipulation of stocks. There are also many other choices available to investors, such as bonds, money-market funds, and real estate. For a public company, especially a reverse merger, to get the investor's attention requires a serious attempt to reach the target audience. You can't just sit back and wait for market analysts to find buyers and hope to make an impact on the market. Financial public relations can help make your day.

## What to Expect from Financial PR

*   Financial public relations can develop exposure for a company's business. It can make the potential investor aware of the company's product, marketing approach, personnel, philosophy, and benefit to the industry. This is not to negate the advantages of advertising, but the costs could be considerably less than the cost of a full-page advertisement in a newspaper or magazine.

*   Financial public relations can provide information to clients, investors, brokers, and analysts, influencing their decisions to purchase or retain a stock.

*   Financial public relations can, over a period of time, develop a favorable reputation for a company, especially if it accurately reflects what the company is doing.

What Not to Expect from Financial PR

*   Don't expect financial public relations to communicate ideas or information about a company's performance, plans, attitude, or potential that don't exist.

\* Financial public relations cannot guarantee that a company's publicity message will appear in a specific media at a specific time.

\* Financial public relations cannot persuade media to run anything but accurate, newsworthy information.

## Making a Commitment

Financial PR requires the same kind of commitment on the part of the president and management of a reverse merger that they give to manufacturing, distributing, and selling the best quality product possible. PR can't be treated as a stepchild. What's more, company management must get involved in the decision-making process of financial public relations if they want it to work. And they must regard the cost, which won't be cheap, as an integral expense of doing business. They must also be able to communicate that positive attitude to the entire company staff.

Let's look at how a few of the major companies regard financial PR. At Reynolds, the public relations staff is designated as an arm of the president's office. At AT&T, the public relations director reports directly to the president. At Standard Oil, the public relations manager reports to the executive vice president. If those successful companies, that some people may feel don't need financial PR, wouldn't make a move without it, shouldn't that serve to convince reverse mergers and smaller public companies of the value of financial public relations?

## Choose a Professional

A professional financial public relations firm is the only way to go. You will get experts at getting the attention of the right people the brokers, underwriters, and investors who can make a difference. Even if a company is large enough to have a full-time person assigned to "investor relations," it's not enough. There aren't enough hours in the day, what with other obligations full-time people get involved in, to implement a comprehensive financial public relations program without outside professional help.

Why short-change the program? Management wouldn't think of doing legal work without engaging professional counsel. It would not, and could not audit its own certified accounting. By the same token, it's much more cost effective and time effective to engage professionals in financial PR. They have established contacts with media and investors; they know how to set up a continuing, consistent, and reliable program.

To make the program work, there must be a commitment between the financial public relations firm and the company. Because what comes out of it reflects corporate policy, insight, and planning.

## Start Early, Stay Late

The importance of establishing an early relationship with a financial public relations firm cannot be overemphasized. In fact, if at all possible, it should be done prior to going public. There's too much at stake for management to put the matter off until later. Hiring professional financial PR can be expensive, but worth every penny in selling out the initial public offering.

Continuing the services of the financial PR firm after the company has gone public is a natural next step, especially through the first year, with a focus on holding and gathering further support for company stock among shareholders.

Of course, an effective financial public relations program extends beyond simply maintaining positive relations with shareholders. Although an outside entity, the PR people will be working as part of the company's management team. Activities should be directed to include employees, potential shareholders, the financial press, analysts, and concerned members of the community, all with an eye on the goal of earning the company the favorable recognition it seeks.

## Where Do You Find Them?

Identifying financial public relations firms is a fairly simple task; finding a good one is another matter and the subject of the following section.

Financial public relation firms, or sometimes referred to as "investor relations," spend a lot of their time with the analysts in the brokerage firms. They wine and dine them, all in the supposed interest of their public company clients. You should inquire of your underwriter—better yet of several—which PR firms they would recommend.

Another set of professionals to ask about for public relation specialists is your attorney. But be cautioned, attorneys often cringe when you start talking about "hyping" your stock. On the other hand, if your securities attorney recommends a PR firm, it gives the firm a lot of creditability as well as reinforces that you have an attorney who understands what public company financial marketing is all about.

## Qualifying the Financial Public Relations Firm

Three basic areas should be evaluated before making a final selection of a financial PR firm. Standard Public Relations Functions

Management should ask the financial PR firm to submit samples of its work as well as recommendations to show that it can perform the job required by management, including assisting and guiding the company in putting together and properly disseminating shareholder letters, press releases, quarterly and annual reports—all with professionalism. It should go without saying that management would expect the firm to familiarize itself with the company's philosophy, people, business, and industry. The public relations people should be expected to prepare an analysis of the market for the product or service. They should also have a keen understanding of the company's position and potential in its industry and know all about the competition and what it is doing.

It is also the responsibility of the financial PR firm to make certain that all written material submitted to management is free of errors in spelling, sentence structure, and punctuation. Management should expect the financial PR firm to be accomplished in writing articles, company brochures, employee newsletters, financial news releases, annual and quarterly reports, employee manuals, external publications, general publicity, press information kits, speeches, and promotional literature; and in engaging in investor relations, press relations, and PR counseling.

Management may decide that some of these areas could be better accomplished in-house or by a regular PR firm. Even so, these are areas about which a financial public relations firm should have a working knowledge.

Management should also be able to call upon its financial PR firm for recommendations about ancillary services, such as market planning, special events, marketing research, finished art, media analysis, photography, catalogs, sales contests, dealer sales ads, industrial exhibits, press tours, marketing counseling, broadcast production, illustrations, media buying, print production, incentive programs, convention planning, direct mail, video presentations, logos and trademarks, packaging, sales meetings, technical literature, letterhead and sign graphics, premiums, slide presentations, and price and parts lists, to name a few. These are services usually handled in-house or by advertising agencies, art services, media companies, broadcast companies, and PR firms. However, a financial PR firm should be aware of the need for these services when they arise and should be able to counsel management and make suggestions.

## Broker Contacts

The street contacts of a financial public relations firm can be of immeasurable benefit to a reverse merger. These could include personal introductions to individual brokers, broker/dealers, financial analysts, and market makers, as well as individual investors. If the choice between one financial PR firm versus another comes down to a toss of the coin, common sense says to choose the one that has the best contacts in the financial community.

It also pays to take the time to personally make contact with some of the clients of the financial PR firm to find out if the CEOs of these companies were satisfied with their broker contacts.

Other information worth seeking out:

* Verify the experience the financial PR firm professes to have in the industry.

* Determine if any of its clients might present a conflict with the company, or if the firms complement each other. If the company is in the computer business, for example, and the financial PR firm represents other companies in the computer business, it may have difficulty finding this reverse merger unique.

* Make sure the firm doesn't have more accounts than it can handle, leaving it without enough time to give the company the kind of service you expect to receive.

* Make certain that the broker contacts are right for the company.

* Look for assurances that the firm is capable of providing on-time service and meeting important deadlines.

## Compatibility

It's extremely important that the financial public relations firm and management are philosophically compatible. Several meetings should give managers an indication whether there is mutual respect and they would enjoy having the firm on their team.

## Summary

Establishing and maintaining a strong, positive financial public relations program can be most important for a reverse merger. The most exciting company in the world can turn into a disastrous reverse merger, if investors are not attracted to the stock offering. It takes determined financial public relations to gain the needed investor attention.

Selecting the right financial public relations firm requires careful consideration. The firm must be professional in its approach, experienced in the industry, and capable of handling all the day-to-day public relations functions you expect.

The right firm will have good broker contacts, and be able to assist the company in its continuing search for qualified brokers and investors. Also important is the ability to plan an aggressive program, reaching out and convincing the greater financial community.

It has been proven many times over that those companies that take advantage of the art of financial public relations, even on a limited basis, are many times more successful than those companies that neglect this vital aspect of corporate life. When used properly, financial public relations can provide a synergism that will enhance total corporate growth and the achievement of the company's financial goals.

# Chapter 12

## DUE DILIGENCE

Due diligence refers to the process that must be complied with prior to an offering being made to the public. The purpose is to ensure that the company has complied with all the legal requirements established by the SEC. This includes examining and confirming that the corporate records, financial statements, and background information about the company preparing to go public are honest and correct.

Part of the due diligence process includes what has often been referred to as corporate cleanup. This could be likened to kicking the tires of a car you're thinking of buying. It amounts to the underwriter-broker/dealer checking out the background of the entrepreneur, the company, and the people who will be running it. This is also the time when the underwriter makes sure that the company is ready to go public and is a good investment prospect for customers. Due diligence and corporate cleanup are interrelated, and as long as they are accomplished, it doesn't make much difference which comes first.

## Legal Responsibility

Actually, the burden of complying with the due diligence process usually falls on the company's SEC legal counsel. It is their responsibility to list, gather, and authenticate things such as articles of incorporation, bylaws, patents, the completeness and correctness of corporate minutes, and other information related to corporate documents. And strange as it may sound, they must also verify that the company exists. Read on:

Part of the due diligence activity of legal counsel must be to make a "familiarization visit" to the company's offices or plant site. And, of course, to charge travel time. More practically, competent legal counsel will assemble a due diligence file that will be maintained for review by the underwriter's counsel, audit accountants, and in some cases, the SEC. It should contain the following information:

1.   Articles of incorporation (amendments) and those of subsidiaries
2.   Bylaws and those of subsidiaries
3.   Annual reports up to five years
4.   Proxy statements and proxies up to five years
5.   Letters from auditors up to five years
6.   Legal counsel letters to auditors up to five years
7.   Distributor and sales representative agreements

8. Listing of representatives by name and original contract date

9. Sales agreements and standard contracts

10. Stock option plans

11. Employment agreements

12. List of materials contracts, names, dates, terms

13. Officer and director questionnaires

14. Any other information management believes would be pertinent

Access must be provided to the following:

1. Minute books of company and subsidiaries

2. Terms of short-term financing agreements

3. Records of long-term debt

4. Copies of debentures and agreements

5. Leases

6. All material contracts

7. Patents and licenses

8. Selling materials for last five years

9. Any other terms, agreements, contracts, or purchases that management may deem pertinent to their business

Legal counsel may also take it upon themselves to perform due diligence in other areas, such as notation of phone calls and written requests in an attempt to substantiate personal resumes and references of the management team. They may perform credit investigation and other background checks on management. They may contact key customers and suppliers and request copies of purchase orders sent to or received by the company.

Most of the above information sought by legal counsel may never be included in their findings. The main purpose for gathering it is to have the information available should it be requested by the SEC.

## Corporate Cleanup

Corporate cleanup could actually be considered an extension of due diligence. Its purpose is to clarify, for the record, corporate transactions that are common in a privately held company. Another objective of corporate cleanup is to assure that the management team remains operative, that it will continue to be in control of the company and work together for its future success.

The process of cleaning up the corporate structure may necessitate the consolidation of several of the company's operations, partnerships, or various corporations that are under the company's ownership and control, which may mean merging them into one corporation. This could become a considerable undertaking—especially for an existing company with a lengthy operating history. Corporate cleanup could also encompass real estate purchases, mergers, acquisitions, liquidations, capital contributions, and stock exchanges.

Another area that commonly falls under corporate cleanup is employment agreements with employees, management, and company officers. This may require dissolving some existing agreements, entering into new or revised ones, changing some of the compensation terms, and even issuing replacement of stock or new stock options.

Cleanup might also involve restructuring loans to or from officers and directors. It could also amount to no more than executing formal promissory notes where none existed before or establishing interest payments that are more in line with present common market rates. If such existing loans were to show bias, they could be found in violation of state laws; hence they cannot be carried into a public company.

Occasionally it becomes appropriate to remove some personal assets that are deemed not legitimate enough to be carried on the company's books, such as resort properties, autos, planes, or the CEO's favorite yacht. Making this information public can pose unwanted tax problems to the principals involved and may require a reissuing of the financial statements. However, eliminating these items from the company books not only saves the company money, but prevents shareholders from charging corporate waste.

Other important areas that need cleaning up before the company becomes public are the adoption of defenses against hostile takeover attempts ("shark repellents") and the limiting of liability, clauses ("golden parachutes"). They would more than likely require changes in the corporate charter (bylaws) or articles in order to comply with SEC rules. In a private company, a simple phone call, a letter, or a lunch meeting is usually all that's necessary to make a change in the bylaws. However, once the company is public these actions require shareholder approval, which could not only take months to accomplish but mean considerable extra cost to comply with the stringent SEC public company proxy rules. Obviously, this process would be less expensively accomplished when there are only a few private shareholders as opposed to hundreds of public shareholders after the company has gone public.

Back to the ever-present concern about hostile takeovers. One way to deter or defeat unwelcome tender offers is to adopt staggered multiyear terms for directors. This assures that the very key directors are continued over extended periods by electing, for example, two directors for three years, two for two years and three for one year at each annual election. This approach is considered a pretty safe shark repellant.

Instituting "golden parachutes" provisions can also serve to protect employment benefits. They can include favorable severance settlements for key management in case of unfriendly takeover or an abrupt change of control by merger or acquisition.

it should be noted that more and more states are approving or revising laws that limit officers' and directors' liabilities. And it is mandatory that the company adopt the most current state laws. A word of advice: A company incorporated in a very conservative state should entertain the idea of reincorporating in a state with a more liberal set of state laws.

Another thing that bears considering is the fact that too many defensive bylaws, such as golden parachutes, turn way some underwriters, especially on larger offerings. Their attitude is that these can make the issue more difficult to sell, as they create suspicion, and therefore make the issue unattractive to public investors. Also, there are a few states that may disqualify the offering as not in compliance with the blue-sky laws. Although smaller companies are not bothered as much by these issues as larger companies, management should be aware of them and should consider the pros and cons with the SEC legal counsel regarding their particular circumstances.

As a safeguard against possible litigation, legal counsel must also be expected to review all contracts for unusual provisions; inspect loan agreements for restrictive clauses; review IRS audits; and examine employee benefits and pension plans for compliance with ERISA (Employee Retirement Income Security Act), which sets standards for retirement and pension accounts. They should also be responsible for checking federal, state, and local compliance on anything from hazardous wastes to zoning.

## Accounting Due Diligence

As mentioned before, strict adherence to due diligence procedures is required on the part of the accountants for a public company. The accountant is responsible for reviewing all purchases, invoices, and canceled checks, and must provide assurances that the company's financial statements are fair and correct. The audit accountants must follow the guidelines of Regulation S-X, which deals with the form and content of financial statements GAAP, and their ultimate certification. They must also comply with the generally accepted accounting principles for presenting audit information. The accountant must then make certain that the company complies with the Foreign Corrupt Practices Act (FCPA), which helped to strengthen accounting standards.

If the accountant concludes that management's internal accounting controls are noticeably weak, due diligence must be intensified or the accountant can be held accountable under the Securities Act of 1933.

The SEC must rely on the validity and authenticity of the accountant's audited financial statements that are included in the registration statement. This puts the responsibility on the accountant to perform a

"reasonable" investigation, and ultimately to provide "comfort" letters (assuring letters) to the SEC and underwriters, which list very specific procedures that have been performed ... and then, all is well.

## Dual Responsibilities

Since a number of areas of due diligence and corporate cleanup can be designated the responsibility of either legal counsel or accounting, a company's management usually has to make a decision as to who does what. For example, both legal and accounting can become involved in pension plans. Lawsuits, warranty disputes, and employee-union relations differences could also involve legal as well as accounting issues.

## Summary

Due diligence and corporate cleanup are considered separate actions, but they are, in reality, part of the same process. Where due diligence investigates the correctness of legal records and the fairness of financial statements, corporate cleanup sets them right. They are, in essence, uncovered by due diligence and corrected through corporate cleanup. Due diligence points the gun, corporate cleanup pulls the trigger. You can't do one without the other.

It is the responsibility of both the legal counsel and accountants to give assurances to the SEC that all regulations have been complied with, that the company going public is a viable company, and that the registration statement and prospectus are correct. At that point, after satisfying the underwriter and the SEC, the selling of the offering can proceed.

# Chapter 13

## LISTINGS

The primary securities trading markets, where a majority of the stocks sold in the United States are listed, are

The New York Stock Exchange

The American Stock Exchange

The regional markets

The Forth Market

The over-the-counter markets

We will be addressing all of these markets; however, in this book we are concentrating on the over-the-counter (OTC) market in particular.

Since the early 1980s, the OTC market has gained overwhelming investor acceptance as a bona fide, legitimate marketplace. In fact, many members of the financial community consider the OTC market as a leader in trading innovations that will go well into the 21st century. It's the exchange where many of the nation's newest and most exciting issues got their start, among them, Microsoft, Apple, Genentech, Intel, and L.A. Gear.

What follows is a look at the markets, their methods of operating, and their listing requirements, which I hope will promote a better understanding of all the trading markets.

## The New York Stock Exchange

In the past, the listing dream and final destination for all public companies was the NYSE. It carried the prestige of being the world's largest and oldest trading place. There are over 1300 members of the exchange, represented by over 500 member firms, and over 150 specialists. This august body is self-ruled by a 20-person board made up of members who own a seat on the exchange. Owners may be corporations, partnerships, or individuals. Membership is obtained by purchasing a seat on the exchange. These seats are limited in number, and in recent years, depending on the profitability of the market (based on investor interest and market volume), the seat prices have fluctuated from $750,000 to $1.8 million.

The exchanges (NYSE, AMEX, regionals) use an auction method of trading (as opposed to the OTC method of telecommunications). This means that an individual, known as a specialist, physically conducts trading activities at a trading post in one particular floor location (exchange). These specialists, or their firms, make a market in one or a group of assigned stocks. Their primary function is to bring buyers and sellers together, and their responsibility is to maintain a fair and orderly market. Specialists match buy and sell orders in their trading books. Only if there is an imbalance in the buys and sells do they trade out of their own account—this is done to preserve the orderly market in a particular stock and to make certain there is continued supervision of this process by the exchanges. During times of large or extreme market fluctuations, such as happened on Black Monday 1987, the specialists' trading system is put to the test. That is also when the value of the auction method of market trading is often questioned.

The NYSE currently lists over 1600 companies trading over 3500 securities. The reason there are more securities than companies is because there are various types of securities. Some companies have more than one of their securities listed and traded, common or preferred stocks, warrants, rights, and options.

## Listing Requirements

The listing requirements for a company on the NYSE are extensive, as is the process. First, an application is made to the Department of Stock List. After the application is approved, it is sent to the SEC for final approval. The listing normally becomes effective within 30 days. The company is then assigned a post on the floor of the exchange. It has no choice or say as to who the specialists will be.

The form for listing is very similar to, and as involved as, a full S-l registration statement. The company is required to keep all its information updated to the exchange on a timely basis. This includes disclosure of information that is of "substantial" character, that is, information that could have impact on the trading of the company's stock. This type of information must be phoned to the Stock List department at the same time it is released to the media so the exchange can consult with the specialists to determine if trading of the stock should be halted. In particular, this pertains to information on:

* Annual earnings

* Quarterly earnings

* Dividend declarations

* Merger and acquisition announcements

* Acquisitions for stock that increase the total amount outstanding by more than 20 percent

* Acquisitions where the stock/cash value paid is more than 20 percent of the fair market value of the company's stock

* Adoption of stock option plans

* Plans for golden parachutes for management or directors

* Shareholders' voting rights

* Tender offers

* Stock Splits

* Changes in top management

* Significant new product developments

* Changes in, or new major contracts

The minimum listing requirements for the NYSE are

* 2000 shareholders

* Publicly held shares with a market value of $18 million

* 1 million publicly held shares

* Income before taxes of $2.5 million

* Net assets of $18 million

* Listing Fee of $51,550

Additionally, the NYSE requires "substantial representation" of outside members on the board of directors and, usually, an audit committee on the board that is made up entirely of independent, outside directors in order to maintain financial integrity.

## Delisting

The delisting requirements are almost as ponderous as for listing on the NYSE. At the top of the list is the failure to meet reporting requirements. Next is the failure to maintain minimum listing requirements, although exceptions are made during the probationary period. A seldom-used reason for delisting is inactive trading of the stock. Also, the exchange can deny listing if there are questionable transactions among officers, directors, or major shareholders of the company. This could pertain to things such as direct or indirect ownership of property or equipment leased to the company, sales or service to the company with interlocking ownership, and ownership of subsidiaries.

If the company requests delisting, it must get the approval of two-thirds of its shareholders, with less than 10 percent objecting.

## The American Stock Exchange

The American Stock Exchange (AMEX) is the United States's second largest exchange, listing about 1,000 securities. It is the world's largest trader of foreign stocks, and the companies listed on the AMEX are generally smaller in size than those on the NYSE. The AMEX is also considered a specialist trading market, very much like the NYSE. However, traditionally, its competitive advantage is that it offers more assistance to its listed companies in the areas of arranging investor conferences, meetings, and research programs.

All of its listing, disclosure, filing, and voting rights rules and requirements are similar to those of the NYSE—except that the minimum listing requirements are less demanding on the AMEX. The minimum listing requirements for AMEX are

* 800 shareholders, 600 of which must own at least 100 shares

* 300,000 publicly held shares

* Publicly held shares with a market value of $3 million

* Income before taxes of $750,000

* Net assets of $4 million

* Bid price of $3

* Listing fee of $10,000

## The Regional Exchanges

Regional stock exchanges serve distinct regions. They are involved with the trading of stocks nationally, but their emphasis is on stocks that have a particular regional interest. Stocks on regional exchanges can also be traded OTC. Now, with the advent of the International Trading System, stocks listed on the NYSE can be traded on any exchange.

Prior to the crash of '29, there were 15 to 20 regional exchanges. One of them, the Boston Curb Market had the reputation of being a famous old playground for skip-shop promoters. These were unsavory promoters who offered phony stocks to the unsuspecting investor and then disappeared with the proceeds. That was a common occurrence among all the regionals during the Roaring Twenties. After the implementation of the securities acts of '33 and '34, along with the establishment of the SEC, regionals either went out of business or consolidated.

By the early 1960s, only eight regional exchanges were still in business. They were in San Francisco, Los Angeles, Chicago, Detroit, Philadelphia, Baltimore, Boston, and Washington. There was also the Cincinnati Stock Exchange, which is regional, but has gone into a computerized system called the Multiple Dealer Trading System. It matches orders and executes them immediately by computer. To improve their business, the other regional exchanges started accepting memberships. Pension funds, banks, and other institutional investors joined as a way of saving on commissions.

By the late 1960s, the need for regional exchanges had diminished greatly. However, there was a growing concern on the part of Wall Street and the SEC over the heavy influence of institutional trading through the regionals. New rules were passed in the 1975 Securities Acts Amendments that effectively prohibited the joint ownership and operation of institutional managers and brokerage firms. Additionally, the deregulation of commissions wiped out the effectiveness of these associations.

Today's regional markets are essentially option trading markets, the most notable being the Chicago Board. The remaining exchanges have consolidated further into the Pacific, Midwest, Philadelphia, and Boston. The listing requirements vary for each exchange, but generally range as follows:

* Net Worth $1 to $2.5 million

* Earnings from tangible to $100,000

* Market float from none to $500,000

* Number of shareholders from 500 to 1000

* Listing fees from $7,500 to $10,000

## The Forth Market

The Forth Market is a recent development encouraged by the continually increasing large stock positions held by institutional investors. These investors consist primarily of pension funds, mutual funds, bank trusts, and insurance companies. Together they have formed a system whereby they execute buys and sells among themselves without the intermediary of a broker. These large block trades are reported to the exchanges, but both the NYSE and the AMEX are seriously concerned about the growing Forth Market. They are trying to devise ways to halt, limit, or supervise this seemingly runaway growth. The computerized and preprogrammed trading by these institutions has come under increasing scrutiny and investigation, especially since Black Monday 1987. The obvious benefit to these large institutions is that it saves them a lot of commission dollars.

## The Over-the-Counter Market

The over-the-counter (OTC) market is subdivided into Pink Sheets, the National Association of Securities Dealers Automated Quotations (NASDAQ), and the National Market System (NMS). Its daily trading function and mechanism differs from the exchanges in that its business is conducted via telecommunications through broker/dealers across the country as opposed to the procedures used by the NYSE and AMEX. The interconnect is via phones and computers, and each broker/dealer provides a bid and ask price for each of the individual stocks they choose to make market in. There are no specialists along the lines of the NYSE, which creates a true negotiated marketplace. The broker/dealers buy and sell on an inventory basis.

Their governing body, the National Association of Securities Dealers (NASD) is composed of broker/dealers themselves. They have a paid administrative staff numbering in the hundreds, located around the country. NASD, as a nonprofit organization, establishes and enforces the regulations for the OTC market. Its chief concerns are

\* To protect the investors from illegal actions by the listed companies and the broker/dealers

\* To establish and implement rules of fair practice for the broker/ dealers

\* To ensure that all broker/dealers comply with federal and state securities regulations

\* To arbitrate grievances or disputes between broker/dealers and investors

## Pink Sheets

The Pink Sheets are so named because they are printed on pink paper over 300 pages measuring 6-by-14 inches. They are printed daily and are available by subscription from the National Quotations Bureau, a subsidiary of Commerce Clearing House. Each trading day's list, which is compiled the previous afternoon from all the market makers across the country, will show the bid and ask price quoted from the market makers.

Pink Sheets are considered to be the OTC trader's bible. By looking up a company by name, the stock, warrant, or bond and the firm that makes the market in each security can be identified. Each market maker's trading line phone number is listed. If the company is on the NASDAQ system, its symbol is also shown.

The first level of the OTC markets are the companies that trade in The Pinks. This includes most of the OTC-traded stocks—over 15,000. Approximately two-thirds of these companies have either chosen not to, or are unable to meet the requirements to trade on the NASDAQ system.

There are actually no listing requirements for the Pink Sheets. If the company is publicly traded with two market makers, it is automatically listed. It is the responsibility of the company's management to secure the market makers and broker/dealers to trade its stock. A broker or trader that wants to trade the stock for an investor would look up the company in The Pinks, identify the market makers, call them on the phone, request quotes and then execute the trade to the customer's best advantage. Confirming paperwork is processed through the broker/dealer clearing system.

## The NASDAQ System

In 1971, the National Association of Securities Dealers (NASD) introduced the National Association of Securities Dealers Automated Quotation (NASDAQ) service and drastically changed OTC trading. NASDAQ is a computer-based quotation/trading system with terminals in broker/dealers' offices all over the country. This system is able to display up-to-the-minute firm quotations.

Today the system is divided into various levels of service. It will show quotes of the best bid and the lowest offer, and the more complex terminals will show all the market makers in each stock, their quotes, last trades in price and amount, and continuous volume. The terminal systems are subscribed to by broker/dealers from NASDAQ.

Over 400 firms are listed market makers on NASDAQ, and the average company trading on its system has eight market makers versus **one** specialist on the exchanges. What's more, the services of the market makers are voluntary, whereas the specialists on the exchanges are assigned. This seems to suggest that the OTC may offer a company better stock trading advantages.

There are also over 4500 companies listed on NASDAQ. The listing requirements are brief and simple:

* A minimum of 300 shareholders
* A minimum of 100,000 publicly traded shares
* Market value of publicly traded shares of $1 million
* Bid price of $3
* Total assets of $4 million
* Total net worth of $2 million
* Two or more market makers
* Listing Fee of $5,000

The maintenance standards for remaining listed on NASDAQ are:

* Total Assets of $2 million
* Net worth of $1 million
* Public Float of 100,000 shares
* Market value of Public Float of $200,000
* Two Market Makers
* Minimum Bid Price of $1
* Minimum of 300 shareholders

A company's stock will be determined to be deficient in its maintenance standards if the issue fails to maintain any of the following individual stated requirements for 10 consecutive trading days: the market value of the public float, the number of marketmakers, and the bid price. Should any failure occur, the company will be notified promptly and will be given 90 calendar days in which to comply with the entry level standard of the specified area failed.

## The OTC Bulletin Board

Additionally, the SEC has instigated a program called the OTC Bulletin Board. This is an "electronic computerized" Pink Sheet trading report. Initial operations have been semi-successful; however, the brokerage community does not like to trade bulletin boarded stocks because of the large amount of paperwork that is required with each trade.

During market trading hours, this computerized system displays the firm and non-firm quotations, and indications of interest in eligible OTC stocks that are not listed on the NASDAQ market.

All Pink Sheet stocks that were listed when the bulletin board went into effect are "grandfathered" as regards their initial eligibility. The decision for determining initial tradability lies with the marketmakers/broker/ dealers. New listing can be instigated, or reinstatement can be made by complying with the SEC Rule 15c2-II.

The Bulletin Board functions very much like the existing NASDAQ system. Each company has a designated symbol on the screen. Firm quotes (bid or ask) are shown, as are non-firm bids, wanted and unpriced entries. Each listing has the name and phone number of the marketmaker who is trading the stock being quoted. The cost for listing is paid by the marketmakers, and is free to the companies. Because of the complications and restrictions in the system,

quotes will be shown on the screens only at trading desks as opposed to screens normally found in a brokerage office.

## The NMS Market

The National Market System (NMS) came into being in 1975 when President Ford signed the Securities Acts Amendments. The purpose was to ensure a national trading structure that would result in a more efficient level of stock trading. It brought stock trading on the OTC to its highest level. It functions through the NASDAQ computer system. Currently it shows trading activity similar to NYSE and AMEX, in that companies that are traded on the OTC NMS show their most recent stock trades, with continuous volume updates throughout the trading day.

The listing requirements for NMS are divided into two categories—developing and operating companies.

Developing companies are required to have a minimum of 800,000 publicly traded shares, $8 million in total capitalization, four years of operating history, and two market makers. The listing fee is $5,250.

Operating companies are required to maintain a public shareholders' base of 300,000 shares, $1 million in operating capital, $300,000 in income, a minimum bid of $3, and two market makers.

In 1985, NMS stocks were granted automatic margin status, which acknowledged full equality with the exchange-listed stocks. This marginable status indicates increased liquidity and therefore attracts more institutional trading. The result has been that an increasing number of OTC stocks are now being found in institutional portfolios because of the high average growth rate of the OTC stocks compared to exchange-traded stocks.

## Public Listings

The company should take advantage of the services of its financial public relations firm to arrange for listings in as many publications as possible. Shareholders should also be informed, on a continuing basis, as to the various publications in which they can find the company's stock quoted.

Most newspapers and financial publications today list the OTC. Its exposure is growing daily. As of now, over 100 daily newspapers carry the NMS and the NASDAQ National list. The Wall Street Journal carries the NASDAQ "Additional List" of over 1800 companies. Many regional daily newspapers also carry a supplemental list of companies that have a regional interest.

Standard & Poor's Index is a widely accepted index of market performance and trends. It includes the price activity of a broad base of 500 leading listed and OTC stocks, including industrial,

transportation, financial, and public utility stocks.

Moody's is an investment rating service of corporate bond issues, preferred stocks, and selected common stocks.

As a point of information, all listed stocks and bonds must have identification numbers. They are provided by the Committee on Uniform Securities Identification Procedures (CUSIP), a NASD agency.

## Broker/Dealers and Wholesale Market Makers

The difference between broker/dealers and market makers can be confusing to the layperson. Generally, a broker will execute a buy through a dealer for his or her client and sell a stock for a client through a dealer—who can also be a market maker (establishes the price). The broker operates on a commission basis, purchasing or selling stock/securities from a dealer. Dealers can also be the persons who make markets on various stocks. Their money is made from the spread, such as on the OTC market, between the bid and the ask price. Although most firms operate in the capacity of broker/dealers, they seldom make a market in all the more than 15,000 OTC-listed stocks.

There are also wholesalers, who are primarily dealers. They make a market (dictate the price of a stock from available information on the stock) and keep an inventory in a number of securities (selling shares of stock that they themselves have purchased for sale). They function in the capacity of dealers to other broker/dealers or to those who are just brokers. As a rule, they have few retail accounts (as brokers).

A market maker is essentially a securities firm that makes markets (designates the price) by always being ready to buy and sell certain securities. They could be brokers or dealers and operate retail or wholesale.

NASDAQ market makers are bound by the rules enforced by NASD, which require them to trade at the prices quoted in The Pink Sheets or displayed on the NASDAQ system. Their quotes must be "reasonably related" (an SEC term) to the prevailing price of the security.

It is usually the responsibility of the company to make certain that there is a market maker for the company's stock. This often takes a certain amount of wining and dining on the company's part. Of course, the market maker prefers to handle a security that shows trading activity. The more trading activity, the more opportunity for the market-making firm to make money on the stock, and the less of a chance of keeping the firm's capital at risk. A good company public relations effort is also important to keep the stock in the public eye. If the price of the stock goes down and the market maker has a lot of it in inventory, the market maker could lose. By the same token, if the market maker has sold a security without having inventory, it must now go out and buy some. In the meantime, if the price has gone up, the market maker stands to lose. Some market makers prefer to stay flat (hold no inventory) on some securities. The names of market makers can be found in the Pink Sheets.

Since market makers wear several hats, it's important for the company to throw in with the market makers whose hats can make the company look good.

# Summary

The OTC market has established itself as the market trading system of the future. Its daily trading function and mechanism differs from the NYSE and AMEX exchanges in that its business is conducted via telecommunications through broker/dealers across the country. The auction/specialists method of trading used by the NYSE, AMEX, and the regional exchanges is slowly losing ground to the OTC market. More and more, institutions are turning to the OTC system. Even England gave up its auction market in 1987 to adopt a system modeled on NASDAQ. Many other European countries are watching this transition closely and are already changing or considering changing their auction markets in the near future. The International Stock Exchange (ISE) is already established, with London being its biggest market. Its Stock Exchange Automated Quotation (SEAQ) system is the international equivalent to our NASDAQ.

With our world's continuing evolution toward an international economy, a computer/telecommunications trading system similar to the one adopted by the OTC market, which can be accessed any time of day, seems to be the only answer. It's no wonder that thousands of NASDAQ-traded stocks that qualify for trading on the exchanges choose to remain OTC.

The listing requirements for the OTC are also less severe than those of the NYSE and AMEX. There are no special listing requirements for the Pink Sheets. Also, where the exchanges use a specialist to conduct trading activities, the OTC uses market makers, which creates a true negotiated marketplace.

Although entrepreneurs first look to the OTC for the reverse mergers targets, it could easily remain their best bet.

# Chapter 14

## THE SEC AND CONTINUING REPORTING

Every aspect of going public is regulated by the Securities and Exchange Commission (SEC). Although mentioned earlier in the book, this bears repeating. The SEC, a quasi-judicial administrative agency of the United States government is responsible for the administration and enforcement of the securities laws. It was created by the Securities Act of 1934, which was passed to regulate the securities exchanges and the over-the-counter market. Pursuant to the Securities Act of 1933, SEC supervises the registration of securities issues and guards against fraudulent sales practices. The '33 act makes all pertinent information about securities available to the buyer.

The commission is composed of five members who are appointed by the president of the United States. Only three may belong to the same political party, and each is appointed for a five-year term. The president designates the chairperson. The commission's staff includes lawyers, accountants, engineers, securities analysts, examiners, and administrative personnel.

There are nine regional offices, located in Boston; Washington, D.C.; Atlanta; Chicago; Fort Worth; Denver; Seattle; San Francisco, and New York plus additional branches through the country. Operations are organized in several divisions:

### Division of Corporate Finance

This division reviews registration statements filed by companies under the '33 act. It furnishes interpretations and advisory services for issuers, underwriters, and their lawyers as to statutes, rules, and regulations. The initial reviewing of registration statements, the major task of this division, is the responsibility of regional branches. Each regional branch is staffed by attorneys, accountants, analysts, and examiners.

## Office of Chief Accountant

This office has final authority regarding accounting matters. It makes policy determinations regarding form and content of financial statements and decides complicated accounting disputes, from consolidated financial statements to Fair Practice Procedures.

Division of Trading and Markets

This division assists the commission and NASD (National Association of Securities Dealers) in the regulation of brokers, dealers, investment advisors, and in securing the cooperation of management of the securities exchanges.

## Division of Corporate Regulation

This division assists the commission in the administration of the Public Utility Holding Company Act of 1935, the Investment Company Act of 1940, and the Bankruptcy Act, and in making sure that the parties involved comply with the regulations.

## Office of General Counsel

This office handles litigation for the commission. It prepares legal opinions and dispenses legal advice on behalf of the commission and its various divisions. It resolves differences of interpretation. It has broad powers and can, for instance, offer immunity on insider trader charges. It serves as a watchdog on international trading.

## Office of Policy Research

This office, headed by the chief economist, analyzes proposals for modification of rules and regulations and prepares statistical data for internal and public publications.

## Investigation and Enforcement

The SEC has the power to investigate complaints about securities violations from the general public as well as from federal and state agencies, and enforce penalties for violations of its rules and regulations. The first step after receiving a complaint is a preliminary investigation. Most investigations are performed by regional offices, with informal interrogation of witnesses. If indications are that a violation may have occurred, the matter is returned to the commission, which can order a formal investigation.

If a formal investigation upholds the charges, the commission considers further proceedings. If the charge is against broker/dealers, the commission may institute administrative proceedings, under the Administrative Procedures Act, aimed toward remedial sanctions against persons or companies involved in the securities industry. The firm may be expelled or have its license suspended or revoked. An individual may be censured and temporarily or permanently barred from employment in the industry. Alternatively, the commission can request sanctions against violators by court order from a U.S. district court. A third possibility, reserved for willful violations, is for the commission to refer the matter to the Department of Justice for criminal prosecution.

## Information Availability

Since the SEC is the primary repository for all public company filings and information, it is obligated to maintain public reference facilities in its regional branches. The SEC is also obligated to provide members of the public with copies of all public company filings at a nominal cost, including opinions of the commission, statements of policy, and interpretations. By law, the commission's decisions, reports, orders, rules, and regulations are always published. A summary of the releases are available by subscription to the daily SEC News Digest (from the Superintendent of Documents, Washington, D.C.). The commission also publishes reports on insider stock transactions.

The SEC staff provides advisory and interpretative assistance to members of the public and prospective registrants. This includes information forms and a list of items available. The SEC staff will also arrange for informal discussions on subjects pertaining to securities.

Continuing reporting is the one thing that public company officers complain about most. According to consensus, it's one of the disadvantages of going public.

Once a company achieves public operating status, it is required to file, on a continuing basis, a stream of never-ending reports to the federal regulators (SEC), and to the shareholders. We will examine the various reports that are required by the government, and we will attempt to shed some light on how a public company can take advantage of these reports by making them reader friendly for distribution to the shareholders as well.

The reports fall into two general areas—legal and public. They must be filed on a timely basis, in formats that do not leave much room for self-expression. They are time-consuming and expensive to produce. The legal side is burdensome. It deals with the requirements that must be complied with according to the rules and regulations of the SEC, the exchanges, and the markets.

The legally required reporting starts immediately after going public and continues at an unrelenting pace forever after.

The optional public reporting leaves room to lighten up and personalize the process. This is especially true as regards annual reports and shareholders' letters. Keeping the investment community interested in a company is no easy task, and it's also expensive.

It is not unusual for a typical small public company to spend as much as $100,000 annually for printing reports and for financial public relations. Continuing legal and accounting expenses could comprise half again this amount. The annual accounting audit is vitally important. It must be reviewed and kept current throughout the year.

Continuing legal advice should also be figured into the budget, as all required reports must definitely be reviewed by legal counsel. Projects such as acquisitions, mergers and divestitures all call for legal expertise to meet SEC requirements. Even press and shareholder releases should go through legal counsel review.

The whole complex matter of shareholder relations, with the preparation of quarterly and annual reports, is best handled by professional financial public relations people. They are familiar with the proper distribution techniques. They have established financial press relationships. And they know who the PR reports should be sent to, such as market makers, individual stock brokers, prospective investors, newspapers, magazines, and broadcast sources. Successful public companies have recognized that continuing reporting is an opportunity to maintain and enhance the value of their stock.

It is management's decision, of course, whether to hire a PR firm on a retainer or strictly on a project basis to produce the quarterly reports to the shareholders, the annual report, shareholders' letters, and other specific PR information.

The quarterly and annual reports should be professionally prepared. The first year's expense for printing and mailing alone could easily run in excess of $10,000. Good financial public relations may seem expensive, but it is an important adjunct to continuing reporting Now, on to the reports:

## Form 8-K: Current Reports

Form 8-K is a report that a company must file when a significant event occurs that could materially affect decisions on buying, selling, or holding stock in a company. The event could be internal or external. The report must be filed no later than 15 days after the event occurred. Timely disclosure rules may also require companies to issue a press release prior to disclosing the particulars that are reported on Form 8-K. Legal counsel plays an important role when reporting on Form 8-K, especially on the interpretation of "other materially important events." Events that are considered significant are

1. Changes in control of the company. This principally refers to changes among persons who control or own big blocks of the stock. For example, a principal of a company could leave the company and his or her stocks would change hands. Or the controller of a large block of stock dies. The public must be advised that there is a change in a big block of stock and management in the company. The requirements are very specific regarding the financial aspects. (See discussion of Forms 3 and 4 and Schedule 13-D later in this chapter; Forms 3 and 4 concern officers and directors of corporations holding 10 percent or more of the stock; Schedule 13-D refers to anyone who acquires 5 percent or more of a company.)

2. Acquisition or disposition of assets. This applies to majority-owned subsidiaries, if the asset value is greater than 10 percent of the company's assets.

3. Bankruptcy. Not surprisingly, this is considered a very significant event. In such cases, instructions are specific that Form 8-K is to be filed immediately after receivership is appointed. All the pertinent facts must be noted, including the court involved, the date of the event, name of the receiver, and date of the appointment of the receiver. An amendment is also required confirming the plans for reorganization or arrangements for liquidation.

4. Change of auditing accounting firm. This requirement is aimed at determining whether the change is taking place because of a policy dispute between the auditing accountants and the company management. For example, management may want the auditing accountant to take a depreciation on a piece of equipment that would not be an ethical procedure. The accountant informs management that it would not be proper.

Management fires the accounting firm. The departing audit accountant files a letter of comment, noting that the departure was not amicable.

This section could also contain an accounting or format change made by a new audit accounting

firm.

5.        Directors. Resignations or the election of a new director are not required to be included in 8-K report. However, if a director resigns and specifically requests the company to disclose the resignation along with the reasons for it, the company is obligated to do so on Form 8-K. A copy of the resignation letter should be attached as an exhibit, and management can include a statement regarding the resignation if desired.

6.        Optional. This is a catch-all for other materially important events. If management and the board want to report a situation of material importance, they must file by the 10th of the month following the occurrence of the event.

The company can report the event or distribute 8-K reports detailing the event to its shareholders. Actually, it seems to be better just to inform the shareholders by a friendly letter or by issuing a press release rather than mailing out copies of the 8-K.

## Form 10-K: Annual Report

This is the annual report that must be filed with the SEC by corporations with more than 500 stockholders and assets over $2 million. It provides an overview of the company's business. It must be completed and filed with the SEC within 90 days after the end of the company's fiscal year.

The 10-K is comprehensive in its reporting requirements. Divided into four parts with 13 subheadings, it calls for audited financial statements with associated footnotes and thorough coverage of the company's operations during the past year. For instance, if the company leased a building, an explanation must be given for leasing the building and a complete description of the building must be included. Also, management must explain what happened, historically, during the year such as, the company introduced two new product lines, started a new subsidiary, signed a licensing agreement in Europe, sold a plant in Chicago, increased the truck fleet, sold off a product line—anything and everything having to do with the company's operations, including sales and marketing.

This report requires the signatures of all the officers and members of the board of directors, so they should all have ample time to add their input and to review it carefully. The SEC attaches a great deal of importance to the 10-K report.

The SEC also encourages inclusion of business projections, which could present a problem. The 10K may be included in the annual report that goes to stockholders. If a projection is not met, it could result in a complaint from an irate stockholder, who may even threaten to sue the company. Therefore, the SEC provides the company a "safe harbor," which allows that projections do not always have to be fulfilled. The company can make them, but is protected as long as it states that these are just projections and may never reach fruition. Many companies refuse to use projections because of the problems they can cause. If projections are to be used, all aspects should first be thoroughly discussed with legal counsel and audit accountants.

Since the 10-K becomes the basis of the annual report, it should be considered a very important document and handled as an important piece of investment communication.

## Form 10-Q: Quarterly Report

The 10-Q is a quarterly report required by the SEC. It contains information similar to that which is in Form 10-K. The report must be filed for each of the first three fiscal quarters and is due within 45 days of the close of the quarter. The main purpose of the quarterlies is to reduce the number of surprises during a company's fiscal year reporting.

Like the 10-K, the quarterly report has specific guidelines. It would be in the company's best interest to secure help from legal counsel and audit accountants in its preparation. Although audited financial statements are not required, there are substantial financial disclosures that must be made. Part I of the 10-Q requires disclosure of the following information:

* Income statement, balance sheet, and statement of sources and application of funds

* A text analysis by management of the quarterly income statement (particularly in reference to material changes)

* Information about capitalization (and changes)

* Information about shareholders' equity (and changes)

The following information, as applicable, must be disclosed in Part II:

* Legal proceedings involving the company.

* Changes in securities. For example, another company may step into the picture to purchase part of the company. It could be issued preferred stock, which would change the basic securities structure. Issuance of warrants would also constitute a change.

* Changes in security for registered securities. For example, the company may have received a large contract and decided to buy back some of the stock. It must declare in this form that it has made an offer to repurchase some stock.

* Default on senior securities.

* Increase or decrease in the amount of outstanding securities or indebtedness.

* Submission of matters to a vote of shareholders.

* Other materially important events.

* Particulars and summary of 8-Ks filed during the reporting quarter. As stated earlier, an 8-K is a current report that provides information on certain specified material

110

events that could affect a decision to buy, sell, or hold stock in the company. It must be filed within 15 days of the event.

The second part of the 10-Q report is not required to be presented to the public shareholders.

The company should think of the 10-Q quarterly report as a natural opportunity to communicate with the investing public and shareholders. The fact that it contains financial statements should make the recipients inclined to read the quarterly report more carefully than if it was just a shareholders' letter. It would also be worth taking a salutary approach to the report by making it reader friendly, rather than simply presenting the cold, hard facts. And since the data is all gathered for the report, management should consider including it in a warm, personal shareholders' letter.

## The Annual Report

After the company becomes public, the annual report is the single most important document the company produces.

Since there are so many publications that deal with the annual report in detail (check local libraries), we will touch only on points that we think are worth remembering.

The annual report is standard reading in areas that are not considered strictly financial, such as customer relations and supplier relations. It is widely recognized as the voice of management reporting on the health and promise of the company. Naturally, it is a vital communication link between management and the shareholders. Therefore, before starting, management should thoroughly discuss the report with legal counsel, the auditing accountants, and the PR firm.

There are two distinct parts to the annual report. The first part is the corporate message—information about the goals of the company and management, which can take up to half the total pages. The second part usually deals with the financial picture.

Preliminary planning should include an evaluation of other annual reports in the industry. Management should have an idea of what they like to see, and what they don't like. The input from other sources, such as underwriters, brokers, and analysts should be solicited. A brainstorming session with the PR firm, designers and printers can be most helpful in determining the overall theme, the style of type, the pictures, the illustrations, and the number of pages that will be needed. Management should be open to suggestions and ideas from these people. (Remember, they have a lot of experience in this area.) A budget and timetable should be determined and adhered to. A decision should be made on the information that will accompany charts and illustrations. A distribution list needs to be compiled.

As to the contents—the company, the people, the products, the programs, and the prospects should be well defined. The chief executive's opinions on important issues, such as strength, growth, profitability, and the promise of the company should be thoughtfully placed and highlighted.

The final product should also fit the company's image. Generally, small companies tend to go all out in publishing annuals, especially their first one. A full-blown, four-color major production may not be the answer—just as simply sending out photocopies of the company's 10-K is not the answer. The underlying purpose of the annual report is to favorably influence the financial marketplace. Everything in the report requires careful planning—and easy reading.

## Corporate Message

The president's report usually leads off the corporate message portion, which is probably the most widely read section of the annual, as readers particularly like to hear it from the horse's mouth. It's the one opportunity for top management to communicate directly with all the owners (shareholders) of the company. It should be composed in a personal, reflective, and intimate style. Here is the president discussing the company's current and future operations.

Here are some key ideas to include:

* History: the company's story, implying in a positive way that the future will be significant and monetarily rewarding.

* Strategy: describing how the company is being run today in accordance with long-term strategies.

* Markets: indicating how the company is competing better.

* Governance: explain how the company is being run by the board of directors to assure survival, profits, and ethicality.

* Future: specifying corporate goals for the next five years.

A photograph or a portrait-style picture of the president would be most appropriate.

## Design

If a picture is really worth a thousand words, good layout and design for an annual report are essential and should be eye-catching. A good design visually holds readers and leads them further into the contents. Consider color, art, photos, illustrations, charts, maps, size and typography; select a good paper stock and cover stock. Headlines and captions are the first things read. In case the reader reads no further, these should encapsulate the whole story management has to tell.

The art director, working with the financial PR firm's creative team, can usually be depended upon to come up with good ideas on the art and photographs—whether they should be stock photos or shot on location; whether to use black-and-white, color, or shaded halftones. Before proceeding, there should be a combined decision on the charts and graphs that best depict the company's operations. The SEC requires specific type sizes and type styles for some parts of the financials. Other than that, allow the creative people an opportunity to suggest underlines, boldfaces, and line spacing. Obviously, there is always a concern for cost with paper. But good quality paper for an annual report must have top priority. Remember, management always has final approval.

As a general rule, small companies print three to four times as many copies as they have shareholders. This policy makes sure there are enough reports to cover the fringe areas—brokers, analysts, requests and media. To further assure that these additional copies get into the appropriate hands, it's important that the mailing list be kept up to date.

A salable annual report requires a great deal of effort and attention to detail by all concerned, including top management. It is important to start planning early—as much as three to four months ahead. But the results can be far reaching and well worth the effort.

## Proxies

Webster defines proxy as "authority to act for another." In the case of a public company management, proxies are a request for shareholders to allow management to vote their shares.

Under state corporate laws and stock exchange rules, most matters that materially affect stockholder rights must be submitted to stockholders for approval. This is done through a special shareholders' meeting. The proxy statement is used to inform stockholders about the nature of the meeting and to

identify the management soliciting the proxies.

Typically, proxies account for a large majority of the votes cast at a shareholders' meeting. Stockholders may withdraw or revoke their proxy at any time prior to a final tabulation of the vote. The proxy, then, is a power of attorney granted by a shareholder for the special purpose of authorizing another individual to vote his or her stock. In most cases, this solicitation concerns the company's annual meeting, which includes the election of the board of directors. For these situations, the proxy package must contain the company's annual report, including the audited financial statements, the names of the directors to be elected, information about them and the management team, and a disclosure of management remuneration.

However, at various times, the company will need to inform its shareholders of other important matters pertaining to the operations of the company. This could be in reference to events such as a major acquisition, divestitures, or stock splits. These are usually information notices and nonvoting situations. In either case, the information contained in the notice must be a description of the matter to be considered or voted on and any pertinent information relating to the matter.

According to SEC proxy rules, derived from Section 14(a) of the '34 Act, all proposed proxy material must be submitted to the SEC 10 days prior to being sent to shareholders. That allows time for the SEC to review the submitted materials for misstatements and omissions. If the SEC has no comments within the 10 days, the proxy materials can be distributed to the shareholders. Proxy materials should not be mailed until this clearance is obtained.

## Mailing

Getting the proxy material to the actual shareholder is no easy matter. Since the late 1970s, there has been an increase in the complexity of the mailing process. First, there has been a large increase in the number of shares held in "street name" (in the name of the brokerage firm on behalf of the owner). In 1975, this included just a small percentage, today, it is estimated at over 55 percent of stock purchasers. Secondly, there is an increasing layer of stock ownership by brokerage firms holding certificates in street name through a Depository Trust Company (DTC),— a computerized go-between for securities transfers that charges and credits each member's account. Thirdly, over this period, there has been a general decline in the U.S. mail service, which, coupled with the fact that the traditional proxy time coincides with the mailing of tax returns and refunds, usually results in the system being overburdened.

Fortunately, most companies have found a way to relieve themselves of this headache. Today, the actual process of mailing, receiving, and tabulating proxies is most frequently handled by the company's transfer agent. Its personnel also attend the annual meeting and, with the help of the secretary of the company, supervise the counting and tabulating of the votes on the issues.

## FCPA: The Foreign Corrupt Practices Act

The Foreign Corrupt Practices Act (FCPA), is a major post-Watergate piece of legislation. It is also deceptively named, especially as pertaining to IPOs. However, the IPO management team should not ignore this act just because it appears, on the surface, to deal only with foreign operations. In reality, it relates to record keeping and applies to all public companies. Failure to comply with its provisions could lead to serious problems.

The FCPA has nothing to do with foreign activities or corrupt practices. It was originally passed by Congress in 1977 because investigations revealed that a certain amount of questionable payments, often illegal, were made by large U.S. corporations to foreign governments, suppliers, agents and customers. Examples cited were improper political contributions, improper overseas payments and the establishment and use of off-balance sheet slush hands.

The FCPA was passed specifically to deal with companies in this country. Part of it prohibits payments of bribes by U.S. companies, their officers, directors, shareholders or agents. Another part deals with two areas that affect a public company's internal controls and record keeping. First, the company must "make and keep books, records and accounts" that detail transactions and dispositions of its assets. This is a statutory accounting requirement in addition to SEC accounting controls. The company must keep detailed records that accurately show and fairly depict any financial transaction involving the company's assets. Second, the company must "devise and maintain a system of internal accounting controls." An accounting control system must be implemented that assures an accurate tracking of all assets and their disposition.

It is important for the company's audit accountants to review the present system and recommend changes, if necessary, to make sure that the company is complying with the act.

## Form 3

Form 3 is a relatively simple report that is filed with the SEC prior to a company's public offering's becoming effective. It requires any officer, or director, holding 10 percent or more of the company's stock to file a statement of ownership with the commission. The same holds true for any other holder of 10 percent or more.

Briefly, the report lists the numbers and types of securities held, the dates purchased, and the method of payment, such as cash or exchange of services, stock, or assets. It describes all stock owned by the individual of record, beneficially (by family members of the immediate household), or otherwise.

It is also necessary, in the event of the election of new directors or appointment of new officers, that a Form 3 be prepared and filed with the SEC with respect to their stock ownership within 10 days of the event.

## Form 4

Form 4 is the continuing equivalent of Form 3. Any officer, director, or holder of 10 percent or more of the company's stock must file with the SEC if any change occurs in the securities owned. Any purchase or sale of the company's stock must be reported on Form 4, including the number of shares, the price, the resulting total ownership, and any other significant related transactions. It applies to all classifications of stock—common, preferred, convertible holdings, rights, options, or warrants, and the conditions under which they were received or purchased.

As with Form 3, the report must be filed within 10 days after the end of the month in which the change occurred.

## Insider Reporting and Trading Restrictions

An insider is anyone with inside information. Using that information specifically to buy or sell securities is considered a form of collusion or fraud by the SEC. Under Rule 1 Ob-5, insiders are those who come into possession of undisclosed material information in the course of their business activities and those who are "tippees" (persons or groups who receive such information from an insider or a third party). These include employees, consultants, retained counsel, accountants, underwriters, broker/dealers, analysts, investment advisors, and those who are informed directly or indirectly by any of these people. Within the purview of Rule 10b-5, they are all insiders.

The Insider Trading Sanction Act of 1984 granted the SEC authority to obtain civil penalties up to three times the amount of profits gained or losses avoided. Liability extends to reporting persons, insiders, and tippees who trade on material nonpublic information.

Naturally, the whole area of insider trading is looked upon with great concern by the SEC. And because it is a complicated and constantly changing issue, it is imperative that management seek legal counsel any time any management team member, director, advisor, or employee wishes to buy or sell stock in the company.

Don't take chances. The SEC has made it very clear that it considers the elements necessary to establish liability for insider trading to be that the information in question be (1) material and non-public; (2) that the tippee who receives the information directly or indirectly, knows or has reason to know that it was non-public and has been obtained improperly by selective revelation or otherwise; and (3) that the information be a factor in his/her decision to effect the transaction (in the security of the company involved).

Under Rule 10b-5, liability could be found even in cases where someone innocently comes into possession of, and uses, information that he or she has reason to believe is intended to be confidential. Such persons can be held liable if, based on such information, they effect a transaction in the securities involved.

## Short Selling

In addition to Rule 10b-5, the reader should be aware of Section 16, which deals with "short swing" profits. This provision applies to any "quick" profits on the company's securities that are realized during any six-month period, whether it's as a result of buying long or selling short. Insiders who profit on those transactions are required to turn over those profits to the company without any offset of losses should they occur. The company can sue the insider, as can any shareholder, on behalf of the company, to recover the profits for the company.

The '34 Act also prohibits reporting persons (those filing Form 3 and 4) as well as insiders from selling shares of stock they do not own—otherwise known as "short selling." "Sales against the box," which is selling "owned" shares but not delivering them within 20 days after the sale, are also prohibited under the '34 Act.

It is very important for the CEO of an OTC-traded public company to establish strong controls to protect the confidentiality of inside information. One help would be to coordinate all press information having to do with news releases and contacts with brokers, analysts and shareholders through one single source. Furthermore, all persons privy to inside information must be made aware of the need for confidentiality and the serious consequences that can come from trading on or tipping that information.

## Schedules

Because of the nature of the Schedule 13s, the reports must be filed with the SEC and with the stock exchanges on which the company's stock is traded or, in the case of

OTC-traded companies, NASD/NASDAQ. The company must also keep complete files on these reports.

## Schedule 13-G

This schedule discloses the names of each person or group who owns 5 percent or more of the company's stock. Within 45 days of the end of each calendar year, they must file a Schedule 13-G with the SEC. This is a relatively simple form, requiring information concerning share ownership with no intention on the part of the owner of changing or influencing the control of the issuer.

## Schedule 13-D

This is considered the takeover alert filing. Any shareholder or group of shareholders who are acting individually or together with the intention of making a tender offer, friendly or unfriendly, must file a Schedule 13-D.

The schedule requires information on the following:

* Identity of the buyer or buyers

* Number of shares owned or controlled

* Dates of purchase

* Source and amounts of funds used to acquire shares

* The reason for the purchase

The alert number is 5 percent or more. As an illustration, if an individual or a group has established a position of 4 percent ownership of the stock in a company, and if that position is increased to 5 percent or more, the SEC regulations stipulate that the holder must file an amended Schedule 13-D. That usually is a clear signal that a takeover will be attempted. There are people in Washington, D.C., whose sole job for their company is to read all the Schedule 13-Ds that are filed to find out if the takeovers will be friendly or unfriendly.

Other 13s that are noteworthy are as follows:

## Schedule 13-E-3

This filing schedule is used by a company if management intends to take the company private or if it intends to reduce the number of shareholders to such a point that the company is no longer required to file the periodic reports with the SEC.

## Schedule 13-E-4

This filing schedule (called an Issuer Tender Offer Statement) is used by companies with securities registered under Section 12 of the '34 Act if they are making a tender offer for their own securities.

## Other Forms and Schedules

The following forms and schedules are listed here simply because they will be required from time to time, and management should be aware of them:

## Form 8-A

This form is used to register securities under the '34 Act. It must be filed immediately upon completion of a public offering, usually in conjunction with S-l 8s that call for registration of securities not to exceed an aggregate offering price of $7.5 million. The form is occasionally used as an optional version of Form 10 under an S-l filing (which is the basic registration form that can be used to register securities for which no other form is authorized or prescribed). Form 8-A is fast becoming obsolete, but it is noted here because the government has not yet eliminated it.

## Form 10

This form is used to register securities with the SEC after a public offering is in effect. Upon filing it, the company becomes fully reporting. All the information needed to complete it can be found in the offering prospectus. It calls for the following items as disclosures:

* Description of the business

* Financial information

* Description of properties

* Securities ownership of officers and directors

* Names of officers and directors

* Executive compensation

* Certain relationships and related transactions

* Legal proceedings

* Dividend information

* Recent sales of unregistered securities

* Description of securities to be registered

* Existing indemnification of officers and directors

* Financial statements and supplemental data

* Difference of opinion with accountants

## Form 10-C

This form, is used only by companies whose securities are quoted on

NASDAQ. It is used for reporting changes in the number of shares outstanding when the change exceeds 5 percent. It is also used to report a name change of the issuer.

## Schedule 14-B

This form is used in the event that there is a proxy contest with respect to the election or removal of a company director. Any person who instigates or is a participant in this type of contest is required to file a Schedule 14-B.

## Schedule 14-D-l

This form is commonly used in takeover attempts. It is used by any person, other than the issuer, who is making a tender offer to purchase securities that would amount to over 5 percent ownership in the company. It must be filed at the time of the offer.

## Form 15

This form is used to officially notify the SEC of the suspension of the responsibility to make periodic filing reports, or it is filed by the company as notice of termination of a registration statement.

## Form 20-F

This form is used only when there is foreign company involvement.

There will, no doubt, soon be more forms to file—as soon as the SEC can think of a reason for them.

## Summary

Continuing reporting makes it necessary for the company to have a thorough knowledge of all the various areas that require reporting.

There are so many forms, schedules, reports, proxies, and restrictions that need to be filed by a public company—it's enough to make an entrepreneur wonder if it is really worth the trouble. Obviously it is. Witness all the reverse mergers that are being undertaken.

There's no getting around it, it takes the full cooperation of the company's SEC counsel and audit accountants to make certain that the SEC receives the reports on time and that they are properly presented. These professional people must prepare checklists of the trigger dates and events to make sure that all the requirements by the SEC are complied with.

The reports should also be well conceived and well written, as a majority of them can easily be used as PR reports for the company, in the form of news releases, press notices, annual reports and shareholders' reports.

The company must just get used to the fact that the reporting is continuous. It never stops—just like the money that keeps rolling in ... we hope.

# Chapter 15

## THE FINANCIAL PRESS

Every day, every week, every month of the year, financial publications across the country pour out stories about the goings on in the financial world. Millions of facts, figures, and interesting bits of information about companies, mergers, tender offers, stock prices, even local, national, and international news items with a financial slant, are tunneled through these publications.

Those stories don't just appear out of the blue, somebody produces them. That somebody is usually a company's financial public relations person or firm.

To fully understand the relationship between financial public relations and the press, one must understand that it is literally impossible for today's financial press to accumulate all those pages of information by itself. The human factor as well as the cost to go around and dig up those stories would be prohibitive. The fact is that much of the financial news that appears in financial publications is fed news—fed by financial public relations firms and by the companies who make the news.

Astute editors of financial publications welcome and rely on fed information to fill their pages. It is the most direct way they have of obtaining reports on items of interest to their readers. Of course, they have their own staffs of reporters, and they do check on the authenticity of a release, but they would be much less effective without the input from financial PR firms. This does not mean that financial publications will accept articles of no particular significance. Any story or release should be newsworthy and of interest to the publication's reader profile, and it should be simply stated. Editors recognize a printable item when they see one. Professional PR people know it is an insult to an editor's professional intelligence to send tout pieces or trivial releases.

Financial public relations, especially in the area of press relations, is an intangible commodity. It is often difficult to measure its effect, success or failure. Because of this, many public company executives are tempted to handle their own public relations. That's a mistake! It takes a professional to do a professional job. Entrepreneurs should ask themselves, Am I a qualified expert in financial public relations? Do I really know the procedures? How well connected am I with the financial press?

When hiring a financial public relations firm, it is most important to choose one that has an intimate knowledge of and a good working relationship with the financial press. Financial publications are forever faced with tight deadlines. Their reporters, writers, and editors appreciate those who respect for and have an understanding of how they work and the standards they must meet.

Financial PR people must also be prepared to verify their sources to the press—to confirm the facts, figures, and content that create the news stories they are responsible for and to provide backup to the stories.

Another significant area of financial PR that companies should seriously consider is buying advertising space in the sections of the press generally titled "Corporate Reports." Almost all the OTC financial publications provide such sections. They are also found in publications such as Inc., Barron's, The Wall Street Journal, Fortune, and others. These are sections where the company can place an ad to advertise itself. The ad could be in the form of a specific favorable report taken from their annual report. Or the company can use the space for a press release, a shareholders' report, or a particular important corporate event, such as obtaining major financing or a valuable contract.

Having a good relationship with the financial press can pay off with big dividends. Here are some guidelines on dealing with business and financial editors:

 * Be impartial—give the news to everyone at the same time.

* Don't pass an old story off as new.

* Don't ask to see a story before it is run.

* Don't expect to be notified if your story is used.

* Don't expect your story to be run as submitted. That's why editors were born.

* Don't be too commercial; if possible, mention your company name only once.

* Don't make exaggerated claims.

* Don't call it news if you ran it as an ad.

* Don't call a news conference if mail will do.

* Don't sit on a story, news is perishable.

* Write for the reader.

When dealing with the financial press, deal directly, honestly, and openly, and you will usually find that you will be treated fairly during good times as well as bad times. Finally, it's worth mentioning again, that every publication has a closing date. If, for whatever reason, the company doesn't get the release or ad in to the publication on time, it's sayonara.

## Summary

Entrepreneurs with dreams of one day being featured in one of those prime financial publications after taking their company public don't have to wait until some distant tomorrow. If their story is worth telling, it's worth printing whenever they're ready to tell it.

A company going public should make every effort to align itself with a creative and knowledgeable public relations firm that has a good working relationship with the financial press.

There are many fine financial publications across the country today, and they all depend on financial PR firms and companies to fill their pages. They are all accessible and willing to work with anyone who has information for the financial world that would be of interest to their readers. Entrepreneurs should not be embarrassed to wave their company's flag. If nobody sees the flag, nobody will know about the company.

# Chapter 16

## MARKET MAKERS

## MARKET MAKERS

Market makers are securities firms that make markets. They stand continuously ready to buy certain securities for their own inventory or to sell securities from their own inventory.

To be more explicit: market makers are broker/dealers. They put their money at risk by buying or selling a stock with their own money, as opposed to brokers who, without putting up their own money, will buy the stock from one source (the market maker) and sell it to another source (a client). They won't buy a stock unless they have a selling transaction lined up. Market makers actually buy the stock and hold on to it until they find a buyer. Many brokerage firms are also market makers, such as Merrill Lynch. They may own stocks from hundreds of companies. Other firms only make market in a few stocks. They are always prepared to buy or sell those stocks at the quoted price on the exchange.

NASDAQ market makers are bound by the rules enforced by the NASD, which require them to trade at the price displayed on the NASDAQ system or the quotes in the Pink Sheets. Additionally, they are forbidden to jump in and out of securities during the day. They must always be ready (at risk) to buy or sell the stock and hold it in inventory. This rule also applies to market makers on the NYSE and all stock exchanges. NASDAQ also requires that the quotations the market makers give or display must be reasonably related to the prevailing market in the security.

Market makers can be either wholesale or retail. Wholesale market makers may have just a few individuals that they make trades for, and consequently, almost all their business is in trading between retail brokers, which is called wholesaling. Ideally, one would expect them to carry large amounts of the company's stock in inventory. On a practical basis, they maintain relatively flat inventories, playing the spreads when the stocks move up or down. Nobody likes getting caught with his or her stocks down.

A retail market maker is the trading department of a retail brokerage firm. Most often it carries inventory to accommodate the brokers in the firm, usually concentrating its positions in securities that were underwritten by the firm. Generally, a wholesaler will make a market in hundreds of stocks, while a retailer will only make market in a couple of dozen.

A market maker actually does more than just hold on to inventory of a stock. Good market makers form a working partnership with the company whose stock they trade to provide the best possible market for the existing stockholders and prospective stockholders. The market-making firm will do this in a number of ways: (1) by assigning an able trader to the company's stock (one who has faith in the company); (2) by furnishing adequate capital to support the market in the company's stock (having enough money available to buy more stock if necessary and also to be able to hold the stock until buyers present themselves); (3) by taking risk positions in the stock and being long or short as appropriate (the market maker tries to equalize the market; if more stockholders are trying to sell, for example, the market maker will take a long position and hold the stock in inventory until the buyers come along; on short sales, the market maker must be able to transact a sell order and buy back later, even if it means losing money on the transaction—what is called covering the short); (4) by providing liquidity for a strong and effective market in the stock (having money ready and at risk); and (5) by acting as a salesperson for the company when talking to securities firms throughout the country (when a retail brokerage firm solicits information about the company for a client, the market maker will provide the information and sell the stock to the brokerage firm). Incidentally, a company can have many market makers.

## Summary

Market makers are indispensable in the trading of a company's stock. They are the ones who, more or less, set the buy and sell prices of certain stocks. Actually, NASDAQ market makers are bound by the rules enforced by the NASD, which require them to trade at the prices displayed on the NASDAQ system or the quotes in the Pink Sheets. They are also bound by rules set by the NYSE and other exchanges.

Each market maker will buy and sell certain securities for and from its own inventory. A wholesale market maker will do almost all of its business in trading between retail brokers. Retail market makers will usually carry inventory to accommodate the brokers in their firm.

Entrepreneurs should make every effort to maintain good relationships with their company's market makers. They must keep the market makers fully informed about the company's operations, including its business plans, financial statements and the special things that make the company look attractive to the investor. They should also try to interest as many market makers as possible in representing the company.

Good market makers are hard to come by. Finding the right ones may necessitate the entrepreneur's catering to their idiosyncrasies and eating a little humble pie from time to time. But the higher the stock goes—the better the pie tastes.

# Chapter 17

## ANALYSTS

Analysts are opinion leaders in the brokerage community. They are usually employed by brokerage firms, banks, and institutional investors such as universities, pension funds, insurance companies, and an increasing number of financial planners. In large Big Board firms, analysts may specialize in just a few- stocks or in a specific industry.

Analysts generally issue reports to the brokers in their firms, who then use them as a guide in advising their individual customers. Most analysts also write or contribute to market letters, which often have a great influence on customers.

On New York's Wall Street:

securities analysts have been called Wall Street's "idea men... financial detectives," and "wizards of odds." They are billed as impartial judges of companies, but their employers increasingly judge them on the trading volume they generate from their recommendations to buy "favored" stocks.

About 15,400 analysts regularly chronicle the daily dramas of America's public companies. Nearly 4,000 work for brokerage houses, spewing out reams of research reports.

Analysts seem to feel compelled to lend their expertise to something that studies suggest they have never been good at—picking stocks that will enjoy immediate glory. They rarely use the word sell in a report, though they may utter it privately. They have a tendency to couch bad news in dazzling, creative phrases. For example, a stock does not collapse in price, it "underperforms the market." Part of their wizardry image stems from the fact that they are often put in a position of making value judgments to determine whether a stock is underpriced or overvalued in its present market price and its near- to long-term investment prospects. It is because of this intuitive aspect of their work that most analysts consider their business to be both a science and an art.

Regardless of what the rest of the world may think, analysts are looked upon as a friend by companies. Management must go out of its way to cultivate relationships with them, to let them know who the company is, what the company is about, and all the great things that are happening in the company. What's more, it should be done on a continuing basis. Out of sight, out of mind.

## The Haves and Have Nots

The problem is that analysts in the low-priced OTC market are a rare commodity. In the small brokerage firms (fewer than 10 brokers), there will most likely not be a designated analyst. Medium-size firms (to 50 brokers) will possibly have someone who functions in the capacity of a combination analyst/syndicate manager. The larger firms (more than 50 brokers) can be counted on to have a full-time analyst.

Unfortunately, analysts in the larger firms tend to concentrate only on the firm's own underwritings. They usually are not interested in small companies. Medium-size firms, who as a rule do not have a preponderance of underwritings, are often open to working on outside stocks, while small brokerage firms can't afford to do much.

## What Analysts Look For

Here are a few items for management to consider, and a few suggestions that analysts brokers, and individual investors should look for in an IPO. The company must present convincing evidence that it meets or will meet the following criteria:

* High and sustainable levels of earnings growth

* High levels of profitability

* Low levels of debt as a percentage of capital

* Solid and improving balance sheets

* Positive cash flow dynamics

* Reasonable market valuations and price to book value relationships

* Dominant positions in small but rapidly growing markets; unique products; aggressive strategies in large, highly fragmented markets

* Management teams that are competent, understandable, and predictable

Another part of the study asks for an evaluation of the management team:

* Who are the members of management, and what are their professional histories and track records?

* Are the business plans and the corporate strategy simple to manage, understand, and evaluate?

* How well does management articulate the business plan and strategy?

* To what extent does management show its confidence in the company by owning stock in it?

* What incentives for good management performance (and penalties for poor performance) does the company provide?

* Does management really accept its responsibility as a public company and treat shareholders as partners?

* Does management scrupulously avoid any conflicts of interest?

## Do's And Don'ts

The report also included a few wise Do's and Don'ts for dealing with analysts:

* Use direct mail.

* Participate in local, regional, and national securities industry conferences.

* Make presentations to analysts' societies.

* Keep the investment community continuously informed.

* Keep management accessible.

* Don't be overly aggressive in corporate strategy.

* Don't overemphasize minor events.

* Don't be overly optimistic in communications.

## Group Presentations

There are not a great many analysts involved with low-priced OTC stocks. Consequently, the OTC entrepreneur should make every effort to cultivate the few that are available.

Occasionally, management is presented with an opportunity to address analysts' societies or social gatherings. These can prove invaluable ways to get the company story to the right ears. Financial PR firms are usually aware of such meetings and can assist in securing an invitation.

If invited, management must decide whether the CEO/president should make the company presentation alone or whether to involve other top executives who possess special expertise. Audiovisual presentations should be considered, or a slide presentation of not more than 15 minutes. Another acceptable form of presentation would be for the CEO to simply extemporize for the time allotted. After all, who knows the company better? It can also be a more intimate presentation.

A common mistake made at analysts' meetings is rehashing volumes of information that is commonly known or easily obtainable by reading existing materials. It can be far more profitable to spend the time telling analysts about future strategies and projections, both short and long term, and give them a feel for the philosophy of the company.

Just for the prestige, analysts prefer to meet the CEO or CFO of a company. Successful OTC companies that have participated in similar meetings know that. They consider it to be part of the strategy in building and maintaining a friendly relationship with analysts.

These meetings should also be followed up by a mailing that includes a financial public relations packet on the company. If the contact seems worthwhile, the mailings should continue. In some quarters, the feeling is that analysts can't do much for the little guys. Well, a lot of the little guys are now big guys because they didn't follow that advice.

## Summary

Stock analysts are people who are considered specialists in analyzing the pros and cons of certain securities by those in the financial community as well as the general public. Their "impartial" opinions are often what make stocks go up and down.

Many of them work exclusively for large broker/dealer firms and dispense their eagerly awaited information to the firm's customers.

Getting a stock analyst to devote time to a small OTC reverse merger is not an easy task. Small brokerage firms simply don't have analysts in their employ, and analysts in larger brokerage firms tend to concentrate on the firm's own underwritings. Entrepreneurs of small reverse mergers do, however, manage to get analysts to do their company. They make the contacts through their broker/dealers or by participating in meetings or conferences attended by analysts. If the company has something going for it, analysts are receptive. It never hurts to try.

# Chapter 18

## THE SHELLS

## SHELLS AND POOLS

The best general definition for a public shell is that it is an "inactive public company." The best general definition for a blind pool is that it is an "artificial shell." Both are backdoor ways of going public, as the entities are, for all intents and purposes, nonoperating public companies. They also come with an existing shareholder base ranging from a few dozen to thousands of individuals.

Shells and blind pools are two other alternatives entrepreneurs can consider in their quest for a public company. They can very well save the taking of lots of aspirins to ward off the headaches encountered in going through an IPO. They can also end up giving more headaches than one would receive from going through the regular process. We will examine them one at a time.

### Public Shells

A public shell is a corporation that has marketable and tradable shares of its stock registered with the SEC and held by the general public. More than likely, it is not currently engaged in any active business operations, and its stock may or may not be currently trading. Additionally, it may or may not be current in the required filings with the regulatory agencies, especially the SEC.

Shells are appealing for many reasons. One is the time and money saved from going through the tedious and costly process of taking a company public. There are also companies that are not glamorous enough to generate public acceptance if they went public. But the owners, for whatever reasons, believe it would be to their advantage to become a public company. The easiest way is to acquire a shell company—a company that was once a public company and is no longer active—is by merging their private company into the shell; they automatically become a public company.

There is an essential difference between going public via an IPO and going public with a shell. Characteristically in an IPO, the public pays a premium for participating in ownership, diluting its investment and increasing the net worth per share of controlling shareholders. In the case of a shell with little or no assets, the original shareholders receive an increase in per share net worth since the shares of the shell have little or no value.

On the liability side, if there are assets, there may be off-setting liabilities, such as a mortgage against an office building. Or there may be debts that have accrued against the shell, maybe from lawyers or accountants, maybe rents that have not been paid, or equipment rentals or loans. Very likely, there will be liabilities and no or minimal assets. These are the things that must be looked into when purchasing a public shell. The reason these things are possible is that public shells used to be operating, publicly traded companies. Many were probably started during some hot market period by well-intended entrepreneurs who had high hopes of heading a successful company.

During the late 1970s and all throughout the 1980s, many of today's shells were oil and gas or other energy-related operations conceived to help solve the country's energy crisis. They were IPOs that raised hundreds of thousands, if not millions of dollars. The companies got caught in the downturn of the energy market, and they floundered. In some cases, management disbanded operations, salvaging what it could by selling off properties for cash. In other cases, the companies kept operating until there was no cash left, and management left. They also incurred debt that may still remain on the books.

The most desirable shells are those with few or no assets, minimal or no liabilities, and little or no negative net worth, with the controlling shareholder base held by only a few people. These people may have been the original founders who have gone on to other endeavors, hoping that one day someone will come along and offer them, if not a profitable buy-out for their control stock, at least a face-saving solution for all investors.

Unfortunately, shells do not end like movies. More often than not, a shell is formed when a publicly traded company fails and the executives who operated it do not dissolve it. In any case, the major problem with all shells is past liabilities. Although those liabilities may still be on the record, in most cases they can be settled. The big question mark comes from the ghosts in the closet, if any. These could be disgruntled shareholders who lie low until new management comes along with cash in the bank and then file suit against the new management for the old management's sins. It is extremely difficult to protect against this kind of action. The best hope is that the investor can be convinced that the new company has great potential to make back the money invested plus more and leave well enough alone.

## History

Shells have been around as long as the public market has existed. They have weathered good and bad reputations. In the late '50s, the SEC prosecuted two notorious shell hustlers named Alexander Guterman and Lowell Burrell. According to reports, these two gentlemen used shells to fleece investors and loot numerous companies. They manipulated stocks by spreading phony rumors to create grossly overvalued market prices and then unloaded their unregistered stock into the U.S. and foreign marketplace.

The same kind of operators are still around, but the SEC continues a careful surveillance, and the abuses are fewer. Today, going public via a shell is recognized as a very legitimate approach. In fact, many shareholders of public companies have no idea that their company was once a shell. There are many honest and dependable shell brokers who have been very helpful in bringing buyer and seller together. Even so, caution is advised.

A study by Alfred D. Morgan* of Southern Connecticut State University attests to the legitimacy and acceptance of going public through a shell. The study points out that an analysis of ads that ran in The Wall Street Journal from 1976 to 1986 showed that the shell market increased fivefold over the 10-year period. The same study also concluded that the supply exceeded the demand by at least three to one.

## Clean Shells

Some shells start out as clean shells. They are brand new. Many of the new ones were first set up in the state of Utah, which has been a continuing source of supply, the work mainly of attorneys, accountants, and other business people. They form a small interstate public company with a few thousand dollars invested in an interest-bearing account. The shell has only a handful of shareholders, who hold on to their stock to "mature" it. The company does not have any operations, it just exists as a public company, or shell. The owners hold it for at least two years to comply with SEC Rule 144, which stipulates that restricted securities cannot be sold before two years from the date they were purchased. At the end of the two years, the owners simply sell control to the new managers, who put their operating company into the shell. The original shareholders profit by selling the stock. They sell enough of it to the new management so that it can have control, but they hold the rest of the stock to sell into the market when the stock starts trading with new investor interest. If the company is successful, they stand to reap a harvest. The advantage of this type of shell is that since it does not have any operations, the liability risk is negligible. The disadvantage is that the company lacks full registration, does not have any market makers, and has a very small shareholder base.

## Advantages and Disadvantages

Every shell has its advantages and disadvantages. There really is not a perfect shell. If it is workable, it fits. The entrepreneur should look into the shell carefully and ask a lot of questions. For example, how financially clean is the shell? What are its assets? If there is cash in the shell, it may become more attractive. The company may need the money to cover the cost of completing the final reports to get the company operating. The company, then, will "buy" the money, but will probably have to pay a steep price for it—instead of getting 90 percent control of the company, the entrepreneur may have to settle for 70 percent control. Depending on the potential price of the stock, that could be an expensive exchange. Also, if there are tangible net assets, do they justify the increased cost of obtaining the shell? On the question of liabilities, the entrepreneur would want to know if the creditors would be willing to discount the debt or settle for stock. Net liabilities or technical bankruptcy do not make a shell unusable.

A shell that is in favor is one that has been around for long enough that the statutes of limitations have run out, thus limiting past liabilities. However, this type of shell can present other problems. Most dormant companies became delinquent in filing reports before they actually ceased doing business. Consequently, all missing reports, quarterly and annual, will have to be updated prior to relisting for trading. The reconstruction of these reports can be expensive and time consuming, and in some cases, make the shell completely unacceptable.

There are also some shells that are not fully reporting. They filed under Reg A or an intrastate filing, so that they did not have to file quarterly reports, only annual reports. A fully reporting company must file quarterly reports as well as the annual report. If the shell was not fully reporting, purchasing it may not be such a good move, as the refiling process could be almost as extensive and costly as doing an IPO.

## Control

The control of the shell must also be weighed carefully. Rather than buy the shell, a company may arrange to merge with the shell. The question is—how to work out the post-merger percentage of control. Here's where the public float (shares held by the public) comes into play. Let us say that 60 percent of the company was restricted stock held by the original owners of the shell. The public float amounts to 30 percent as a result of the IPO. Private financing owns the 10 percent balance and the original owners can't decide whether to sell the new company 90 percent of their 60 percent or just 30 percent or 40 percent of it. They decide instead to issue more shares, which dilute the percentage of the public float, and give them and the new company the lion's share of the outstanding stock. Now the public stock may be down to 5 percent to 10 percent of the total outstanding shares, which is too small a public float as far as brokerage firms are concerned. It means that the inside shareholders have too much control. Should they decide to trade two years hence, when they can sell their 144 stock, it could drive down the stock price. The actual control percentage is the obvious number that the new management is concerned about. They will ultimately want majority control of the outstanding shares. Many shells are acquired in multiple stages. A second acquisition could be conducted shortly after the first, with additional shares issued to the principals, thereby giving them control. There are many ways to obtain and then retain control, including the issuance of different classes of common or preferred stock. These should be discussed with the SEC counsel and accountants to be sure that all areas are covered concerning the total shares publicly or privately held and the new management's holdings. Many of these problems can be avoided by simply starting out in full control of the shell.

## More Questions to Ask

* What was the company's product or service? Could use of the product result in liability lawsuits?

* What was the trading history? Did the stock have wild price fluctuations that may have caused disgruntled shareholders?

* What is the status of the founding second-round shareholders? Are they willing to sell out their original shares at a reasonable price or, at minimum, will they be cooperative in the timing of selling their shares back into the market?

\* Were there any second- or third-round original investors that need attention now to prevent future problems?

\* Did the original company do any desperation, late-round financings that could carry forward added liabilities? (Late-round financings can take the form of preferred stock or subordinated debt.)

\* Are there any outstanding options, rights offerings, or warrants? Are there any underwriter's warrants outstanding? (These usually extend for four or five years after the original effective date of an underwriting.)

An ideal shell could also be a company that is currently operating whose management wants to take it private. This is usually a no-asset, no-liability, currently reporting, very clean situation. If the shell in question is currently trading, questions to ask are:

\* Who are the market makers, and how many are there?

\* What is the current stock price, and what was the last year's or last active trading period's history?

\* Is there a current list of the brokers that maintain positions in the stock?

\* What is the current status of all required SEC reports, including 10-Ks, 10-Qs and 8-Ks?

\* What is the status of state and local reports?

Note that there are no questions here about tax-loss carry-forward. The government canceled that in 1986. It used to be a big perk for entrepreneurs obtaining shells. For example, Ms. Entrepreneur buys a shell that shows $1 million in losses. She would put her company into the shell and she wouldn't have to pay taxes on the first million dollars she made, because she had a tax-loss carry-forward. Under the 1986 Tax Reform Act, tax loss is virtually useless for mergers or shells. At best, only a small fraction is retainable.

## Shareholders

There is a definite advantage in having a large number of shareholders on the books of a shell as opposed to just a few, as there are in new shells. Poplar consensus is that 300 to 1000 is an ideal number, showing that there is a large enough base of stock out there to get the market makers interested in trading it. Fewer than 300 may not show enough public float. But more than 1000 can create excessive shareholder contact expense for a new company. All those shareholders must be communicated with when the trading is reactivated. That comes to a lot of letters and reports that must be sent out.

Compiling all the shareholder names can also be a problem. A lot of stock today is held in street name through brokerage firms, which makes it difficult to get a firm handle on the number of shareholders. It requires direct contact with the brokerage firms to determine the actual figure. Also, dormant companies usually have outdated lists, which make it even more difficult to reestablish contact. But it is important to get to these shareholders.

Most reactivated shells have a base of shareholders who purchased the stock at substantially higher prices than the reactivated trading price. Consequently, they rarely sell out immediately. Instead, they wait until the stock has, at minimum, regained its purchase price. This is a great opportunity for management not only to hold these existing shareholders but to encourage them to make additional purchases and become faithful to their born-again company. The fact that the existing shareholders now own stock at higher prices can create new buying that can move a stock price up dramatically.

## Finding a Shell

The OTC market and the National Securities Dealers Pink Sheets are good places to start the hunt. Hunters look for stocks quoted at pennies, often with no bid, and only one or two market makers. But these factors can also be misleading. It's possible that the company in question is just marginally profitable, with thin market trading, and management has more interest in perpetuating salaries than producing shareholder returns.

A more fruitful method may be to watch ads in the financial press, contact broker/dealers, or make a direct contact with a shell broker. Most broker/dealers do not get involved in the purchase of shells directly, but they will refer inquiries to finders.

Finders, or shell brokers, make it their business to seek out shells or distressed companies that most likely will become shells. Their fees are negotiated, and often include retention of stock. They can give a prospective purchaser a feel for current market pricing. Many shells are controlled by individuals who may or may not have a realistic value established as to the worth of their holdings. Then the purchase price becomes a major bargaining point.

## Cost of Shells

There is no set off-the-shelf price list for shells. Prices can range from $20,000 to $100,000 and up. Many variables come into play including: the amount of control, cleanliness of the shell, net assets, board control, number of shareholders, and reporting status.

## Acquiring a Shell

There's more to acquiring a shell than meets the eye. A number of steps must be taken. Here is an example:

1. The new management team purchases control of the shell by buying stock from the existing controlling shareholders.

2. They then set up a new, wholly-owned subsidiary of the parent company, whose only asset is the parent company's stock.

145

3.      The subsidiary acquires the private company in exchange for the parent company stock, thus increasing control by the new management group.

4.      Since the parent company owns 100 percent of the subsidiary, it then votes an upstream merger with the subsidiary (takeover).

The result is that the parent company has merged with the private company without going to the shareholders for approval. At this point, an information statement should be sent to shareholders and ratification of the action is usually put on the agenda at the next shareholders' meeting.

Basically, this has been a simplified approach to shell acquisitions. The purpose is to leave the reader with a fundamental understanding of how shells work. Even with this understanding, it is not wise to acquire a shell without the help of qualified legal counsel. One reason why Rule 144 came into existence was the abuses that occurred in shell combinations. Be aware that the SEC continues to tighten its requirements for proxies and other filings concerned with shells.

One more thing of interest about shells. They seem to run in cycles. When the number of IPOs go down, interest picks up in shells.

## Spin-off Shells

Until the mid 1960s some existing public companies created subsidiaries for newly formed operations and spun off a portion of the subsidiary's stock to their shareholders as stock dividends. The result was that a new public company was formed without the need for registration. Subsequently, if the subsidiary did not perform well, the parent company enjoyed a residual value by selling the subsidiary's controlling shares. A deliberate abuse of this loophole caused many spin-off shells to be created. The SEC stepped in and started challenging these spin-offs when, in its opinion, there was no justification for their existence.

In the mid 1980s, the spin-off syndrome started again. Today, the merit review process of many states restricts the percentage of "promotional stock" issued—that is, stock issued at no cost to the shareholder. Consequently, registered distribution of stock and warrants by way of spin-offs is again receiving the careful attention of the SEC and regulatory bodies across the country.

## Blind Pools

Blind Pools are similar to shells ... only different. They have, at times, been considered the first phase of a shell. They are offerings in which participation money is raised, but the investment or company is not identified. The investor depends on the expertise and integrity of the blind pool founders to make the investment pay off.

Blind pools were first conceived in the oil and gas industry. As the story goes, a group of successful oil men wanted to prospect for oil. They realized it would take more money than their finances would allow. So they approached investors to invest in them blindly, without their even knowing themselves where they would drill or how they would spend the money. It was called a blind pool. Blind pools have also been referred to as blank check companies and artificial shells. Many have been used as a means of bringing needed financing into an existing operating company. These companies often turn to blind pools because underwriters didn't feel that the companies presented a glamorous enough image and therefore didn't show interest in an underwriting. In essence, they are publicly traded, often not fully registered shells, with cash. Their corporate charters are written in broad language to allow the companies to engage in all lawful activities. Investors put their money into these companies, often without knowing who runs them or what they are going to do with the money.

Blind pools were further encouraged by the 1980 Business Development Company Act. This federal legislation eased the Investment Holding Company rules designed to promote small business. They came into modern day prominence in the mid 1980s in the Rocky Mountain region, primarily in underwritings by the small OTC firms in Utah

147

and Colorado. From 1984 to 1988 the percentage of blind pool underwritings rose from 5 percent to 65 percent of the total underwritings.

## Abuses

In the early '80s, a lot of fast-buck operators abused the system. By mid 1986 the SEC had charged 32 blind pools with violating securities laws. Charges included:

* The use of undisclosed principals, major shareholders, and investors

* Having prearranged mergers set up

* Insufficient disclosure of conflicts of interest

* Issuance of cheap stock to promoters

* Unjustified salaries to founders

* Bonuses to finders

* Misuse of proceeds

Additionally, the SEC stepped up surveillance of broker/dealers with attention on market manipulation, churning of customer accounts, investor suitability, trading spreads, and financial disclosure.

In the late 1980s, the states of Utah and Colorado revised their securities regulations to effectively stop new blind pools in their states. This was accomplished by requiring all blind pools to escrow a large percentage of their proceeds until an acquisition was identified, and then all shareholders were allowed to vote on the proposed acquisition.

## Unit Offerings

As promoters became more sophisticated in the assembling of blind pools, they recognized that they had to raise the ante. They began to offer acquired companies more than the standard $50,000 to $500,000 they had been offering. This resulted in the unit offering. The new stock was now sold in units of common stock and warrants.

A unit was priced at 10 cents and consisted of one share of common stock and two warrants—an "A" warrant exercisable at 15 cents and a "B" warrant exercisable at 20 cents. Some of the warrants had qualifications. The "A" warrant was good for one year, and the "B" warrant was good for two years.

The concept behind the unit offerings was that if the company was successful, the price of its stock would increase and consequently the investors would exercise their warrants with the company.

As an example, the initial offering would yield gross proceeds of $500,000, assuming the offering was for 5 million shares (units) at 10 cents. A year later, if the company had been successful and its stock was trading at 18 cents to 20 cents per share, the shareholders would exercise their warrants, bringing $750,000 into the company (5 million "A" warrants at 15 cents each). The second year the process would be repeated with the "B" warrants, bringing in $1 million (5 million "B" warrants at 20 cents). Thus one blind pool underwriting could easily total $2.25 million in proceeds to the company over the two years.

Many variations to this approach have been put together, with some unit offerings having as many as four or five warrants.

## Warrants' Exercise

In theory, the concept of warrants being attached to a blind pool is a good idea. In practice, it has presented many problems. For instance, the original units are often issued in one of two ways. One is as an attached unit, where the warrant stays attached to the common stock. The other offers a detachable warrant, where the warrant is separated from the stock and trades by itself. The bookkeeping, or tracking of the detached warrant holders, can be a transfer agent's nightmare.

149

In either instance, attached or detached, the responsibility to get the warrant exercised is the company's. Some companies prefer to contact the warrant holders directly to remind them it's time to exercise their warrants. Others prefer the lead underwriter to handle the chore. Either way takes a lot of effort and precise tracking to obtain successful results.

What makes the task seem so thankless is that most investors in blind pool units view the investment strictly as a gamble. Consequently, the dollar amount of their investment is usually small, maybe $500 to $2,000. Their hope is that the stock price will quickly increase 50 percent to 100 percent, and they can "turn out" for a quick profit. The bottom line is that the original investor is usually not interested in any further investment in the warrants.

There are also rules that apply to warrants:

* A purchase warrant simply offers the holder a right to purchase a specific amount of stock at a specific price, exercisable at a specific time.

* The exercise price can be reduced but cannot be increased.

* The shares underlying the warrant must be registered, which requires the company to file a post-effective amendment. (This filing is equivalent to a full S-18.) The reason behind the SEC requirement for such an extensive update filing is that the whole nature of the company changes when a merger with a blind pool occurs. In effect, the company loses its privacy.

## Costs

The cost of acquiring a blind pool is comparable to the cost of a shell. It can vary from $10,000 to $200,000 and up. The process usually requires the company to purchase control positions from the founding control shareholders. The deal often includes sizeable options for additional shares for the founders.

Some blind pools are set up with differing classes of stock in order to assure that management will control the voting rights. They would sell common stock with no voting rights to shareholders and preferred stock with voting rights to management to give it control. The original founders use these inside stock positions as bargaining points.

## Hidden Costs

A major deterrent to becoming involved with a blind pool is the eventual total cost to complete the whole deal. Audited financial statements are a specific requirement. First, audited financial statements are required from the private company shortly after combining with the blind pool. Then audited financial statements will also be required of the combined companies. There are also legal fees and filing fees to be paid for the immediate and continuing reports.

The entrepreneur must realize up front that purchasing a blind pool does not relieve the company from the reporting requirements of a publicly traded company. A lot of blind pools will have met only minimal reporting requirements, so getting the new blind pool company up to full reporting status may require just as much time and dollar expenditure as it takes to accomplish a new IPO. Which, of course, takes us all back to the beginning of this book.

## Summary

For the entrepreneur, going public through a shell or a blind pool is a legitimate way to achieve public company status. By definition, a shell is an inactive public company. In many cases, by buying a shell, the entrepreneur can save a lot of the time and money it would take to go through an IPO. In other cases, it may take more time and money than starting an IPO from scratch just to bring the shell up to fully reporting status.

Some shells have assets that can be absorbed. Some have liabilities, and often these liabilities are not obvious. They can crop up later by way of suits by disgruntled owners

151

of the former company's stock or through debts that have been accumulated. It requires sophisticated advisors who are familiar with the legal, accounting, and regulatory pitfalls of shell acquisitions to make the right choice. But a good shell can be a shell of a bargain.

A blind pool has been referred to as an artificial shell. It is a publicly traded, often not fully registered shell—with cash. Unlike a shell, which at one time may have been an operating public company, a blind pool is not. Many investors consider a blind pool a gamble. It can also cost more to bring it up to a fully reporting public company than does an IPO.

Stock ownership of shells and pools have the same high leverage potential that is sought in any public company. And like a shell, a blind pool is an expedient way of going public, if not gone into blindly, of course.

# PostScript

The next step may be the most difficult, most nerve-wracking, most anxiety-ridden, most agonizing step an entrepreneur could take ... which is going public.

It's alright to dream about it, but to be honest, the door to the dream won't swing open simply by your saying "Open sesame." It takes more than just a few magic words or rubbing lamps. Actually, rubbing is involved—rubbing hands, rubbing heads, and burning a lot of midnight oil. But it's not an impossible dream. Stories abound about entrepreneurs turned multimillionaires because of taking their companies public.

As I have repeated throughout this book, our focus has been on the reverse merger. The rewards are well worth taking a company public. There are pitfalls associated with reverse mergers, but a far-seeing entrepreneur will find that the benefits easily outweigh the negatives. There's no trick or special secret to the process. Going public is a process in which a business owned by one or several individuals opens its doors to public participation by offering the public an opportunity to invest in the company. Everything that must be done to go public is spelled out in detail by the government for anyone who is interested.

However, to protect the innocent investor, the government has established rules and regulations. A lot of them. I've discussed most of them in this book. I touched on some things, and I went into depth on others, among them—the importance of timing; the need for advisors and consultants; the way to find the right legal and accounting people; the advantages of private financing; finding and dealing with underwriters, market makers, and brokers/dealers; and the necessity for good PR. I presented alternative methods for going public and deluged you with a lot of rules and regulations.

Of course, one reading alone will not allow you to retain the thousands of essential points that have been covered. However, your base familiarity with the book's contents will allow you to use it as a continuing reference source. It can serve you as a manual of techniques, systems, and guide points to give you assurance and assist you in meeting your goals.

Going public is a heady as well as a heavy experience. I hope that after you accomplish it, you will share your experience and expertise with others. Teach them, mentor them, use your organizational skills and leadership gifts to help them and to encourage them. Pass your tenacity on to those who can benefit from it.

This book hasn't given you the experience. However, when you do it yourself, you'll find it has furnished you with the knowledge you'll need. You've learned that timing is important, that you need to be prepared to take advantage of the windows. You've learned that there's a lot yet to learn. As John Case, the senior editor of Inc. magazine said, "When the investment bankers aren't tripping all over themselves to take companies public, is precisely the time to study up on the subject."

You understand that selecting the best professionals to assist you is important. You have learned that it is possible to effectively work within the guidelines of regulators. You have also studied the world of underwriters. You know the registration process.

Building a company is a dynamic process. It takes a continuing, unrelenting, and committed attempt to create value. You must strive to achieve new insights, encourage innovation, pursue excellence—excellence in your product or service, excellence in your management team, and excellence in customer results.

The rewards are achievable. They're significant. They can feel good—both in your pocket and your heart.

My entrepreneur's wish to you is that this book has helped you gain the confidence you need to go after it—to capture the dream.

Printed in Great Britain
by Amazon